THE SECRET POWER OF KRIYA YOGA

THE SECRET POWER OF KRIYA YOGA

Revealing the Fastest Path to Enlightenment.

How Fusing Bhakti & Jnana Yoga into Kriya will Unleash the most Powerful Yoga Ever.

- REAL YOGA BOOK 2 -

SANTATAGAMANA

Copyright © 2017 by SANTATAGAMANA

All rights reserved.

1st Edition, December 2017

ISBN: 978-1981122639

Version 1.3 – Updated July 2018

Special thanks to Eric Robins, who edited and proofread this book with profound love, kindness, and dedication.

No portion of this book may be reproduced in any form, including photocopying, recording, or any electronic or mechanical methods, without permission from the author except for brief quotes.

Cover art: pitris/Bigstock.com & vvadyab/Bigstock.com

Disclaimer for Legal Purposes

The information provided in this book is strictly for reference only and is not in any manner a substitute for medical advice. In the case of any doubt, please contact your healthcare provider. The author assumes no responsibility or liability for any injuries, negative consequences or losses that may result from practicing what is described in this book. Any perceived slights of specific people or organizations are unintentional. All the names referred to in this book are for illustrative purposes only, are the property of their respective owners and not affiliated with this publication in any way.

Read also, by the same author of *The Secret Power of Kriya Yoga*:

— **KRIYA YOGA EXPOSED** [REAL YOGA BOOK #1]

The Truth About Current Kriya Yoga Gurus & Organizations. Contains the Explanation of a Special Kriya Technique Never Revealed Before.

— **KUNDALINI EXPOSED** [REAL YOGA BOOK #3]

Disclosing the Cosmic Mystery of Kundalini. The Ultimate Guide to Kundalini Yoga & Kundalini Awakening.

— **THE YOGA OF CONSCIOUSNESS** [REAL YOGA BOOK #4]

25 Direct Practices to Enlightenment. Revealing the Missing Key to Self-Realization. Beyond Spirituality into Awakening Non-Duality.

— **TURIYA: THE GOD STATE** [REAL YOGA BOOK #5]

Unravel the ancient mystery of Turiya - The God State. The book that demystifies and uncovers the true state of Enlightened beings.

— **SAMADHI: THE FORGOTTEN EDEN** [SERENADE OF BLISS BOOK #1]

Revealing the Ancient Yogic Art of Samadhi.

— **THE YOGIC DHARMA** [SERENADE OF BLISS BOOK #2]

Revealing the underlying essence of the Yamas and Niyamas. A profound and unconventional exposition on the spirit of the Yogic Dharma principles.

— **LUCID DREAMING: THE PATH OF NON-DUAL DREAM YOGA** [SERENADE OF BLISS BOOK #3]

Lucid dreaming like you've never seen before. The complete alchemical elixir: Transform Lucid Dreaming into Non-dual Dream Yoga.

Available @ Amazon as Kindle & Paperback.

Subscribe and receive the ebook **Uncovering the Real** plus updates and information regarding new books or articles, which will be sent about once a month.

www.RealYoga.info

If you have any doubts or questions regarding this or any of the other books, feel free to contact me at:

Santata@RealYoga.info

When one abides in the Parvastha of Kriya upon having performed Kriya, one is the Self-Knower.

- Lahiri Mahasaya

Guru Gita, commentary by Lahiri Mahasaya

TABLE OF CONTENTS

Introduction 13

Part I - The Dawn of a New Understanding

   1. God is the True Siddhi 19

   2. Fake Gurus and Detours 23

   3. Breaking Free from the Ultimate Spiritual Dogma 27

   4. Do I Need a Guru? 35

   5. What Kind of Kriya Practice is the Best? 39

   6. Searching Everywhere but Ourselves 45

Part II - The Real Yoga

   7. The Blasting Fire of Kriya Yoga 53

   8. The Art of Non-dual Bhakti 71

   9. The Miracle of Jnana Yoga 77

   10. Where is Karma Yoga? 83

   11. All Yogas are One 87

Part III - The Forgotten Stairway to Bliss

   12. Saving the World 93

   13. The Abysm of the Intellect 95

   14. Expanding Parvastha Holds the Keys to Infinity ... 99

15. The Secret that No Kriya Yoga Guru Will Ever Tell You   105

16. Giving Up the "I"   111

17. The Yogi, the Bhogi and the Sage   117

Part IV - Transcendence

18. The Mysteries of Samadhi Unveiled   123

19. The Absolute Beyond Comprehension   135

20. The Lightless Light in the Depths of Darkness   141

Resources   **147**

Glossary   **149**

Introduction

This book reveals the fastest path to Enlightenment.

No more detours, distractions and lifetimes. It is *now* that we are going to do it.

We will be turbo-charging your Kriya practice beyond the unimaginable, by adding the supreme wisdom of Jnana Yoga and the pure love of Bhakti Yoga into the super potent fire of Kriya Yoga.

If you are willing to be open to what is taught in here, the result will be mind-blowing.

Kriya Yoga was made known to the public en masse after the publishing of *Autobiography of a Yogi* by the great Paramahansa Yogananda.

Yet the goal, Self-Realization, is still missing for most people. Why is that? What is missing here? What is the missing link?

To transform human consciousness, we must introduce something new, not the same old Kriya story over and over again. Do not expect to find superficial and common Kriya teachings in this publication. We've had enough of that already.

This book will introduce that *something new*. The teachings herein are undoubtedly unique for most Kriya practitioners and to those who endeavor to reach the Ultimate Reality, the Supreme Freedom. This is especially true since most Kriya practitioners' minds have been brainwashed by organizations, gurus, traditions, and Kriya literature in general.

This book exposes the direct yogic path, without unnecessary pages full of useless information that is not relevant to your awakening and Self-Realization, leaving no stone unturned.

Most Kriya Yoga books are marketing baits to lead you to an initiation or organization. Not this one. This publication is a call from you to you, without intermediaries.

This volume shows something completely different, something that really makes a difference. Something that will help people experience pure bliss faster. Something that will help people attain eternal Freedom quicker. Something that doesn't require one to be meditating in a cave for fifty years in order to *achieve* Self-Realization.

We don't need more dogmas, we don't have more time, and we definitely don't need more ego distractions. What we need are enlightened beings. What we need is light. What we need is love. What we need is to recognize our true nature.

This book contains only that which is most essential. It answers the most relevant Kriya questions like "What kind of Kriya Yoga is the best?" or "Do I need a Guru?"

All chapters are infused with Kriya, Bhakti and Jnana Yoga energy and teachings, with quotes by Masters from all of the three paths.

Nowadays, Kriya Yoga is enveloped by duality. This work will help you to break free from that, toward the Oneness, or better said, the Aloneness (*Kaivalya*). For That which Is, is neither two nor one, but simply IS beyond our limited understanding of "being."

This book will share teachings no other Kriya Yoga book ever shared. All the *Samadhi* mysteries will be revealed, plus a secret that no Kriya Yoga Guru will ever tell you.

It is time we go further and deeper into consciousness and find out our true nature. As we explore the Secret Power of Kriya Yoga, by unifying Bhakti and Jnana Yoga with it, the most fantastic things will happen, such as the surging of peace and happiness never known before, accompanied by a clear realization of this universe's true nature as a dream-like creation. Whenever we open our mouth, Consciousness itself will speak the words of non-dual wisdom precisely as the ancient Sages did. Unalloyed bliss will be our heart's permanent song.

After exposing Kriya Yoga in the first volume of this collection, *Kriya Yoga Exposed*, we will now unleash its tremendous power as the basis for all Yogas to come into fruition, going beyond our apparent existence and mortality, into the realmless realm of the Absolute (*Parabrahman*). That is our destination, going faster than light, faster than anything conceivable, into the inconceivable beyond nothingness.

Do you dare to go that deep inside?

Are you ready to unlock all the secrets of the Universe and Existence?

You are. Because you are already It.

Here and now you will recognize your forgotten infinity.

1
THE DAWN OF A NEW UNDERSTANDING

CHAPTER 1

GOD IS THE TRUE SIDDHI

Many people start practicing Kriya Yoga after reading *Autobiography of a Yogi,* by Paramahansa Yogananda. It is a very inspiring work.

Although most people love it for its miracles, display of *siddhis* and marvelous stories and experiences, it's actually a love story between a man and God. His search for God and the truth is what is inspiring.

You must know what your motives are. Why are you practicing Kriya Yoga or any spiritual discipline? Be absolutely honest with yourself.

If you are practicing Kriya Yoga to achieve supernatural powers, to have nice experiences, to be able to do out-of-body projections, to impress others, to acquire wealth or fame, and so on, you must know that you will fail.

What do I mean by fail?

You might be able to achieve those superpowers, develop clairvoyance, perform miracles, do "astral projection" and visit other realms at will, or even manifest all of the wealth and worldly success you desire, and you will surely impress others. But you will fail at being Free. You will fail at being enlightened. You will certainly fail at being One with God.

The problem is not the powers, abilities, experiences, wealth, etc., for those can come (and go). The issue is only in your surrenderness, your genuineness, your true deepest will.

There was an interesting conversation between Ramakrishna Paramahamsa and his disciple, Swami Vivekananda, where Swami Vivekananda complained that all of the disciples except him seemed to have gained superpowers or had visions. Ramakrishna Paramahamsa merely replied "That is good."

This might sound like a weird reply, but bear with me: why do people want those supernatural powers? Why do people want those occult abilities? Why do people want to manifest an epic life? Why do people want material wealth?

It is because they believe those *things* will make them special, complete and happy.

Whatever people wish for is just because they believe it will make them happy. What they are looking for is happiness!

God is the pinnacle of happiness. God is peace and bliss beyond belief. That's the goal of humanity, that's your goal—to be eternally happy, to be blissful beyond what you can imagine. That is being One with God, which is the purpose of all Yogas.

God is not an entity or a form. That would make God limited by your perception and consciousness. God is formless; it is your own consciousness. The difference is that your consciousness appears to be limited (ego-consciousness), while God is infinite Consciousness (Self-Consciousness).

All misery comes from fear, from unsatisfied desire. When we find our true nature, when we find God, we will have no more fear, we will no longer be unhappy. That is Freedom.

If any superpower comes to you, that is perfectly fine. Is there any problem with using it? No. Unlike what other Gurus may say, "God" will not punish you or anything like that. The only thing that might happen is a distraction or a detour from the direct path to enlightenment. It is indeed a delay, but not a crime.

If you understand that what you want is to be happy, and that the only reason you want to achieve an occult ability, mundane success or any other externally-oriented goal is because you believe these things will bring you happiness, then you will not desire them anymore. You will only wish for perfect happiness, perfect bliss, perfect peace and perfect ecstasy. That is God. That is you. Your true nature is pure unbounded happiness.

> "Ever-new Joy is God. He is inexhaustible."
>
> - SRI YUKTESWAR GIRI
> AUTOBIOGRAPHY OF A YOGI

Usually, when it is taught a way to empower the individual or to increase the sense enjoyment, we find lots of interested people. However, when it is taught how to achieve the supreme goal for humanity, nobody seems to care about it. Few have the genuine desire to realize the highest truth, and fewer still have the self-sincerity and patience to attain it. This is exclusively due to their lack of discernment. They are also looking for that happiness, and think a "successful life" will bring it. But we are not going to settle for a temporarily successful life. We are going for the most auspicious goal.

This is the reason you are practicing Kriya Yoga or any other spiritual practice. You want to be eternally happy.

Come and sail beyond the ocean of birth and death, of mundane existence, into the inexhaustible everlasting joy, the Supreme Existence.

CHAPTER 2

FAKE GURUS AND DETOURS

In my previous book, *Kriya Yoga Exposed*, I talked at length about Gurus, organizations, and their teachings. We have seen that most Gurus teach truths intermixed with dogmas.

Organizations might be beneficial for beginners, explaining the techniques, showing them how to do practices correctly, etc. The issue is that this also comes with incorrect and ego-based teachings.

Unfortunately, finding beliefless Kriya Gurus seems to be rare. Many of them have been culturally influenced by the most varied superstitions, and were taught Kriya with lots of discipline and austerity. If that seemed to work for them, they will teach it exactly in the same way. This is how a tradition works and how a lineage continues.

We will not go that route. We will abstain from any cultural influences, superstitions and austerities. We will not be confined to one organization or to a specific set of practices. In the beginning, we must search and choose what works for us, but this cannot be an excuse to keep seeking over and over again, Master after Master, organization after organization. That nomadic type of pursuit is just an ego trick to keep us in the realm of the search. We must find what works and keep practicing it exclusively.

This book is the end of that search, by combining what works from all Yogic traditions, and removing what doesn't work or is too slow. We are only interested in the most potent, fastest spiritual practices, and have no time for distractions or detours. I will not ask you to stop practicing what you practice or to stop following your Guru or organization. You can simply incorporate what is taught here into your practice and life.

Many Gurus add extra practices to the ones that work so that they seem more complicated and more complex. The mind likes complex things and will love a set of highly technical procedures like some Higher Kriyas are.

An intricate maze of practices lasting multiple hours is not more efficient than a simple Pranayama done over and over again. Lahiri Mahasaya, the father of Kriya Yoga, advised his most advanced students to practice around six hundred

Pranayamas and fifty Mahamudras and nothing else. How simple is that? How straightforward is that? How powerful is that?

If you have read *Kriya Yoga Exposed*, you know that it is *not* about the techniques themselves. It is all about the "After-Effect-Poise of Kriya," otherwise known as *Parvastha*. The goal of Kriya Yoga is to effortlessly be in that state.

If we can reach Parvastha in a faster, easier and more straightforward way, why would we waste hours and hours with complex procedures? Let's do what is simple, natural, and stunningly effective.

The Self, our goal, must be ever-present. If it is something we have to reach and keep, then we can lose it as well. If the goal is ever-present, then it must be present *before* realization, *during* the spiritual practice, and *after* realization.

It is precisely like silence. Silence is ever-present, although it seems to be temporary, due to noise. When we shut up, silence is there. We didn't reach it or gain it; it is simply there. When we liberate ourselves from the limited and wrong ideas we have of who we are—of being this person, this body, and this mind—we will recognize that our real blissful nature is ever-present. Even in the midst of noise, silence is still present as the background that allows noise to be. Even in the midst of life, our true Self, our happiness, is present!

Remove all the noises, and only Silence will be.

Remove all the mind-noise, and only pure blissful Consciousness will be.

It always ever is, we just need to recognize it. That which allows everything to be, That we are. It is beyond concepts, beyond description and guess what, beyond practice.

CHAPTER 3

BREAKING FREE FROM THE ULTIMATE SPIRITUAL DOGMA

Throughout your journey as a Kriya Yogi, or even as a practitioner of other traditions or methods, one thing you will for sure encounter: dogmatic teachings.

These dogmas come in many forms. Some are based on the tradition itself, like restrictions or penances. One that we hear about frequently is, "If you don't eat *sattvic* food, you will have no chance at spiritual success."

Don't get me wrong, I eat *sattvic* food, but it was not due to some imposed rule. My body has naturally chosen to eat a purely vegetarian diet. This is how it should be, never forced. The known Yamas ("don'ts") and Niyamas ("do's") from the *Yoga Sutras* should be consequences resulting from your practice, rather than imposed or forced restraints.

There is a known story where this is clearly demonstrated. It is about a conversation between Paramahansa Yogananda and a new disciple, where the latter asked:

"Guruji, all my life, I heard thou canst not [you cannot], thou shalt not [you should not], thou must not [you must not]. These are the rules of the religious teachings that I've heard around my relatives. What I want to know from you is, what canst thou [can you]?

"Well, do you smoke?" Paramahansa Yogananda asked him back.

"Yes," said the disciple.

"You may continue," replied Paramahansa Yogananda. "Do you drink alcohol?"

"Yes."

"You may continue. Do you enjoy the opposite sex promiscuously?"

"Yes."

"Well, you may continue."

"Wait a minute," said the disciple. "You mean that I can come up on this hill here, in this good place with all these wonderful people, your disciples, the devotees, the brothers up here and study these teachings, and I can go back down there and do all these things?"

"Absolutely," said Paramahansa Yogananda. "But I will not promise you that as you continue to study these teachings, that the desire to do these things will not fall away from you."[1]

> "Knowing That which survives the annihilation of 'I' is alone the true Tapas [penance]."
>
> - SRI RAMANA MAHARSHI
UPADESA UNDIYAR

Another form of dogma is based on the personal journey of the Guru. For example, if he or she says: "I have practiced Kriya Yoga for 30 years, 10 hours per day. I know this approach works and I know that you must do exactly as I did if you want to succeed."

That's fine. My question is:

Why not do it faster? Why do you have to practice for 30 years before *achieving* enlightenment? Is the Self only on the other side of a physical or mental activity?

---

[1] From "Awake: The Life of Yogananda" (2014)

> "Many teachers will tell you to believe; then they put out your eyes of reason and instruct you to follow only their logic. But I want you to keep your eyes of reason open; in addition, I will open in you another eye, the eye of wisdom."
>
> - Sri Yukteswar Giri
> Man's Eternal Quest

Enlightenment is like death. It takes one single instant to die, but a long life usually precedes it. It also takes one single instant to be enlightened, but a life (or many) full of spiritual practice usually precedes it.

Now the most important question we need to investigate is: What is the best way to reach that precise instant?

There are people who have reached it faster (way faster than 30 years), and those who have practiced for a long time but didn't reach it (way longer than 30 lifetimes). Shall we limit it to a question of karma?

This brings up a huge debate: free will vs. karma. Which one is stronger, which one wins?

Can someone who is genuinely seeking liberation actually liberate him/herself, or will his/her karma put up a huge impenetrable wall?

> "If we are the doer of actions, we will experience the resulting fruit. However, when we know ourself by investigating who is the doer of action, doership will depart and all the three karmas[2] will slip off."
>
> - SRI RAMANA MAHARSHI
> ULLADU NARPADU

The "I-ego" is the seed and base of both karma and free will, since it alone has free will and experiences karma (destiny/fate).

The central choice we have is between keeping our attention and involvement in the external (*pravritti*) or withdrawing back within and abstaining from being part of the mind's projections (*nivritti*).

As long as we appear to be this "I-ego," karma will seem to exist and to be directing our life. However, if we earnestly practice, go deep within, and never give up, we will discover that we are not this "I-ego," and are therefore completely untouched by karma.

---

[2] The three types of karma are:

1. *Agamya* - a new action that we do of our own free will, which we will experience its fruit at a later time;

2. *Sanchita* - The store of our past karmas that are yet to be experienced;

3. *Prarabdha* - The karmas that we will experience in this lifetime.

> "Since all effects or seeds of our past actions, our karma, can be destroyed by roasting them in the fire of meditation, concentration, the light of superconsciousness, and right actions, there is no such thing as fate."
>
> - PARAMAHANSA YOGANANDA
> KARMA, THE LAW OF COSMIC JUSTICE

Be persistent, and you will have the realization that you have no karma. Karma belongs to the body-mind only, and you are beyond it. Like Sri Ramana Maharshi once said: "When there is no 'I' there is no karma."[3]

Yoga usually also comes with the belief that there is an individuality (*jiva*) that is separated from the universality (*Shiva*), and there must occur a union.

Let's stop for a moment and consider:

Did that separation ever occur? The jiva might appear to exist, but does he *really* exist?

Instead of starting from the paradigm of being a jiva and having to be one with Shiva, we will start from the *knowledge* that we are already Shiva. We just have to recognize it! That is a huge difference.

---

[3] The Teachings of Sri Ramana Maharshi, edited by David Godman.

If you were something external to God or separated from God, that would make God limited and finite; He wouldn't be omnipresent, all-pervading.

This makes no sense because God, pure Consciousness, must be infinite and incorporate everything, both the formless and the form. If we equate formless consciousness with H_2O, and ice, water and vapor with forms, we can see how H_2O is their basis and is unseparated from them. If God were apart from you, why would you want to merge with Him? Why would you want to merge with something limited (as it doesn't take into account yourself)? That would still mean you'd be lacking absolute completeness.

With the knowledge that we cannot be separated from God, we can then realize that we must be God. If we are God, why do we suffer, why do we feel like an individual, why are we not eternally happy?

This is due to the veil of Maya, the illusion. This is the veil we have to unveil, by self-recognizing our true Self as being God (Shiva), rather than having to unite with Him, for now we know we are not separated from Him!

This knowledge destroys the biggest dogma of all: the belief that we are this limited consciousness that has to expand and unite with the infinite Consciousness.

It is with this new awakened discernment that we will go forward. We are not trying to become one with God anymore. We already are God but we just don't seem to remember it. Let's walk this illusory path of removing the imaginary veil that doesn't let us recognize this Ultimate Truth. We are God, and we have never been anything else, for nothing else truly exists.

Kriya Yoga's starting point has been changed. It now starts from the *Advaita* point of view of non-duality, rather than the yogic duality. This is a new beginning, and although it might seem to make a small difference, it makes a big difference.

> "Dualism is the root of all suffering."
>
> - LAHIRI MAHASAYA
> LAHIRI MAHASAYA'S DIARIES, AUGUST 1874

It is not a "me into God" or "me and God" journey anymore. It is a journey-less journey of One that has never been two.

CHAPTER 4

DO I NEED A GURU?

Yes. Everyone needs a Guru. The Guru is *that* which takes you from darkness (ignorance) toward light (enlightenment).

Having said that, the Guru is not limited to a physical body. Everything is your Guru, including life, since it is constantly making you turn inside. Suffering and unhappiness also have the single purpose of making you stop and look deep within.

The Guru can be external but is always internal. Internally, it can appear at first with a form, according to your tendencies and predispositions, and as you go further into the depths of your own being, it will be revealed to be formless, to be your own consciousness.

Now, when we talk about a human Guru, things must be approached differently. If we are talking about a genuine Guru, one who has liberated him or herself from the veil of illusion, that is a huge help. Someone like Sri Lahiri Mahasaya, Sri Ramana Maharshi, Ramakrishna Paramahamsa, Adi Shankara, and so on. I'm not even talking about the oral teachings (which can be life-changing), but just by being in their powerful presence, lots of *vasanas,* negative tendencies and desires would definitely dissolve. If you can find a Guru like that, it is priceless.

The problem comes when many gurus claim to have *reached* enlightenment, when in fact they have not. They might have gone deep in meditation, and an aspirant who visits them might feel some energy, *Kundalini* activations, have visions, etc., in their presence. These gurus might even exhibit *siddhis* which are very impressive (to the ego), but we will know, if we have sharp discernment, that some of their teachings just cannot be right. A big warning sign is when their teachings are fueled by a heavy dose of dualism.

The true Guru is the *Satguru,* the inner Guru, God, Self, or whatever other name you wish to give it. This Guru has been guiding you, silently, toward your liberation. "He" is the same as all of the true physical Gurus, for their real identity is the formless infinite Consciousness that can appear in any form.

Sri Ramana Maharshi used to say that the body-mind of a Guru is still an illusion, but an illusion that can wake you up.

It is like a lion appearing in an elephant's dream. It is powerful enough to wake the elephant up from the dream.

There are so many quotes by Lahiri Mahasaya that unquestionably show that the true Guru is the Self, and I've documented many of them in *Kriya Yoga Exposed*.

> "Self is the one and only Guru."
>
> - LAHIRI MAHASAYA
> SPIRITUAL COMMENTARY ON KABIR

Why do we still cling to the outer Guru so much then? Because we still identify ourselves with our body-mind. As long as we consider ourselves to be this piece of flesh, we will have the limited idea of being this "I."

Our true Consciousness appears to be clouded over by our profoundly engrained desires and tendencies of attending to otherness, such as thoughts, forms, external objects, etc.

As we usually keep our awareness extroverted, toward things that we imagine being other than us, our real Self has to appear externally as well, in a human form. This happens so that we can learn from him/her by words, energy, presence, and so on, empowering us with the understanding of the true nature of the Self/Reality, and showing us the path by which we can *achieve* it.

When we correctly follow the teachings of the Guru in human form, we will turn our attention inward, toward being, toward consciousness, discovering the inner Guru. The true formless form of the inner Guru is our own consciousness, which was previously concealed by our mental noise.

Nonetheless, Grace is not restricted to a specific space-time. For instance, even though Paramahansa Yogananda dropped his physical body, his Grace will still be with you if you are genuine and practice Kriya Yoga with truthful motives. You don't even have to belong to the organization he founded. If you are his sincere devotee, he will not reject you, even if you stop practicing the Kriya as is currently taught by that organization, or if you slightly upgrade some specific practice. Believing that his Grace is exclusive to members of the organization he founded is absolute sectarian nonsense and a mere religious dogma. Do not let such illusions brainwash your mind.

All true Gurus' Grace and guidance are as powerful and real now as they were when those Gurus were in their human bodies. They are ever-available, ever-present and ever *pulling* us back to our common source, the Self.

CHAPTER 5
WHAT KIND OF KRIYA PRACTICE IS THE BEST?

The best Kriya practice is the one that takes you as quickly and easily as possible to Parvastha, which is a state of blissful Self-awareness.

If you could achieve that Samadhi state with one single Pranayama breath, why would you want to do 500 of them?

If you could achieve Liberation just by snapping your fingers, would you do it, or would you rather do 10,000 Pranayamas? Are you interested in the goal (God/Absolute happiness, peace and completeness beyond understanding) or in the techniques or lineages?

Techniques are just a tool, not the goal. The *technique-is-god* mindset is so typical in Kriya Yoga that practitioners forget the real purpose. Never shall we forget that our true Self is the goal.

Let us imagine that there was an ultra-fast, uncomplicated way that would enlighten you. All that you had to do was to smile at five strangers. That's it. So simple, and it would instantly *give* you enlightenment.

Would most people do it? No. Not even the people who say that they want to liberate themselves from all suffering and achieve eternal happiness.

Most of the people who do spiritual practices, study spiritual books, and so on, would not do it.

Why?

Because most people are too attached to their lives, belongings, ideas, beliefs, etc., and are not willing to let these go. I don't mean leaving your family or home and going to live alone in a cave; I mean breaking the attachment. All of your attachments will have to be let go of when you leave your body. Why not drop them right now?

People would come up with multiple false reasons not to smile at five strangers. Their desire to keep their illusory self and world alive is way stronger than their desire for eternal Freedom.

"It's too simple, it will not work."

"It's too complex, it will not work."

"It's too weird, it will not work."

"Most Gurus don't teach this way, it will not work."

"If it were this easy, everyone would be enlightened by now."

All that would be needed was to just smile at five strangers, but instead their minds rationalize excuses for not doing it. Perhaps they are just not interested in Self-Realization and prefer to have only an intellectual understanding. Most are just pretenders. They prefer an innumerable flood of thoughts or experiences that would pose as signposts toward Realization. Don't be fooled.

Ultimately, if your current Kriya practice is not giving you results, if you feel like it's going too slowly, or if it's not a joyful moment anymore, be honest with yourself. Having self-honesty is a tremendous help. Don't keep doing the same thing over and over again and expect it to give you different results.

Perhaps those techniques are just not for you, or their results are too slow, or it could be that the issue is not about the techniques themselves, but on your motivation or your degree of surrender.

The best spiritual practice is one you love to do, one that gives you happiness and peace. Kriya Yoga unmistakably does that, unless you approach it mechanically or in a "dry" way.

This book is teaching you exactly how to approach your Kriya practice, how to give it a huge boost to go beyond the conventional teachings into the "faster-than-light" territory, awakening true non-dual wisdom.

Although Kriya Yoga is often given in a group-initiation in a general way, and marketed as a "mathematical formula toward God, such that no matter who is doing the practice, it will work 100% of the time", this is not quite right.

Kriya is not supposed to be an en masse instruction. Lahiri Mahasaya gave instructions on an individual basis according to the temperament and maturity of each disciple.

Paramahansa Yogananda, on 29th November 1935, went to Sri Ramana Maharshi and asked him: "How is the spiritual uplift of the people to be effected? What are the instructions to be given them?" Sri Ramana Maharshi answered, "They differ according to the temperaments of the individuals and according to the spiritual ripeness of their minds. There cannot be any instruction en masse."[4]

Initially, some base instruction must be given, and the practitioner should follow it to the letter. When enough intuition has been developed and recognized, one should allow some space in the Kriya practice for spontaneity.

---

[4] Sri Munagala Venkataramiah; *Talks with Sri Ramana Maharshi* (2013).

That doesn't mean you suddenly switch up all your practices. No. But imagine you are doing some Pranayama, chanting Om in the Third-eye, when suddenly a strong urge to mentally chant Om in the Crown Chakra arises. Let your attention gently go upward to the Crown Chakra and chant Om there. These things happen for a reason and your consciousness knows precisely what to do. It's just an intuitive icing on the cake, not remaking the whole cake.

If you follow the teachings of an organization or Guru, and you ask them about making changes based on intuitive guidance, they will most certainly disapprove of it and say: "Just follow the instructions as they were given to you. Refuse everything else." They are just playing it safe. In that situation you must decide whether to listen to your intuition or not, and the best way is to follow your heart. Some *schools* go even further and say "If God came to you and said: 'Give me your hand, and you will be enlightened' you should refuse His invitation, ignore Him, and go back to the mighty technique we taught you." Don't let other's delusions be your own delusion.

Let your Self guide you toward itself. Melting in the lap of God is the best spiritual practice.

CHAPTER 6

SEARCHING EVERYWHERE BUT OURSELVES

"We can know God only by knowing ourselves."

- PARAMAHANSA YOGANANDA
THE SCIENCE OF RELIGION

Every time we are doing a spiritual practice, we are focusing our attention on an external object. In our Kriya practice, we start by focusing on breathing, prana, chakras, mantras, physical movements, etc. Eventually, we will awaken the Kundalini and experience multiple higher states of consciousness, which will culminate in a Samadhi. That will be a blissful experience, but then your normal ego-consciousness will return, and in the long run, little will have changed. Many become frustrated trying to repeat that experience, but to no avail.

We can have lots of visions, ecstatic states, hear astral sounds, meet "ascended Masters," or any other kind of beings, but all of this will always be temporary and will not *get* you enlightened.

> "Only what is eternal is worth striving for."
>
> - SRI RAMANA MAHARSHI
> THE TEACHINGS OF RAMANA MAHARSHI

An experience will always be temporary. Are you looking for something temporary? Or are you looking for what is eternal? And what is it that is eternal? Not the body, not a chakra, not a vision, not the life-force nor even the mind. What is eternal is beyond all of that, beyond time.

Have you ever experienced anything beyond time? Is there any moment where time is just not there? What about when you go to sleep and wake up four hours later to go to the bathroom, and can't believe four hours have already passed? Yes, you were not experiencing time during those four hours because your mind (the experiencer of time) was submerged in Consciousness (deep dreamless sleep state). We call it unconsciousness, but if it were unconsciousness, we would never know that there was a "blank," a nothingness period between dreams. That is actually very similar to

Nirvikalpa Samadhi or *Yoga Nidra*, only that we are not acceding it consciously. If the mind is not present during such periods, but there is a base consciousness empty of everything, then only that pure empty Consciousness meets such criteria. That is our goal.

Our attention is always on external things, even focusing on a subtle perception like a chakra or the life-force is still an external attention, an attention to an "object." The only way attention can be internal (objectless attention) is when it is focusing on itself, reposing as Being, as Presence.

Your empty consciousness, without any objects, is internal. Everything else is external.

When we wake up, the first thing that happens is that we gain body-awareness. Then, we notice where we are, the objects around us, the external world, etc. Being aware of all these things is only an external attention.

Until we go to sleep again, our attention stays externalized, experiencing every object of perception through either the five gross senses or the five subtle senses. When we fall asleep (deep dreamless sleep), our externalized attention terminates.

From the moment we wake up until the time we go to sleep, from birth until death, from the creation of the universe until its dissolution, all living beings keep their attention externalized. No one ever redirects it back to itself, to the background of consciousness. People are so hypnotized by Maya's movie that they do not even notice the screen-consciousness upon which the movie is being projected.

Now we know that we have to turn our attention around 180° degrees and focus on consciousness itself. That is what the Parvastha state, the "After-Effect-Poise of Kriya" is. It is merely the mind paying attention to itself, to emptiness. Practicing Kriya Yoga speeds up this process of attaining a deep Parvastha state.

> "When the mind does not go in other directions—when the mind remains in the Mind—the mind is purified."
>
> - Lahiri Mahasaya
> Guru Gita, Commentary by Lahiri Mahasaya

> "If the mind stays within the mind by the practice of Kriya, then one achieves the speed of Speedlessness."
>
> - Lahiri Mahasaya
> The Commentaries' Series Vol. III: Hidden Wisdom With Lahiri Mahasaya's Commentaries

Do not worry if initially, emptiness might appear to be "nothing." If you keep at it, spaciousness, bliss, and peace will surge up from within pretty quickly.

In the beginning, this might be quite difficult, for the mind's noise will not let you do it. That's where Kriya Yoga comes in. We will still the mind and awaken the latent energy (Kundalini) by practicing Kriya Yoga, and we'll unify it with Bhakti Yoga, because real love, devotion, and surrender boost anyone's practice beyond belief. Meanwhile, we will also practice Jnana Yoga and start some intense inquiry within, breaking the wrong identification with what we are not, awakening the essential discernment and non-dual wisdom that are necessary for true awakening. This is not just limited to a "conventional sitting practice," but also includes reading or hearing words that directly convey the Truth without dogma (like this book). Such direct pointers are crucial.

The final stage of practice is the expansion of the potent cocktail of Kriya's Parvastha and Jnana's *Atma-Vichara*, which are one and the same. The only difference is that while we are brought to the first one through our Kriya practice, the second one is consciously induced and *maintained*.

With the combination of *right knowledge*, a quiet mind, and love-surrender, the Parvastha state of Beingness will be easily and strongly accomplished. Everything will come out of this state, or better said, this state will melt away everything until only consciousness is left. We will not do this in sequential phases, but instead will start with the three Yogas all at the same time, in different degrees. With practice, we will increase the potency of each part. When it is done correctly, as prescribed in this book, it will shorten the duration of your path from decades or lifetimes to some months or years. It all depends on your earnestness, degree of surrender, and genuine desire.

Unless you really want to attain true Freedom, all of the inner changes will be superficial. Don't let the fear of ending the ego prevent you from having an intense desire for Self-Realization. It's your highest purpose.

Now is the time to awaken to who you *already* are.

2
THE REAL YOGA

CHAPTER 7

THE BLASTING FIRE OF KRIYA YOGA

There are many different ways of practicing Kriya Yoga. Each Guru and organization teaches its own version, most of them claiming to be the "Original Kriya," while others declare their method to be the "Airplane route to God."

Since we have already seen that we are not separated from God, but are only removing the illusion of such, we are not concerned with any "Airplane route to God."

> "I have lived on the lip of insanity, wanting to know reasons, knocking on a door. It opens. *I've been knocking from the inside.*"
>
> - JALALUDDIN RUMI
> THE ILLUMINATED RUMI

We've been knocking at the door of God's Temple, but we're actually knocking from inside!

Regarding "Original Kriya Yoga," since we already learned in *Kriya Yoga Exposed* that Lahiri Mahasaya taught different versions to different people in order to suit their temperaments, maturity, and tendencies, we are not concerned about being the "Original Kriya Yoga" either. That would be an endless endeavor. What we are concerned about is doing the practices that take the least possible time and effort, and yield the strongest results.

In the previous book, we talked about five main Kriya practices[5]:

Khechari Mudra (with the introductory Talabya Kriya)[6], Kriya Supreme Fire, Mahamudra, Kriya Pranayama and Yoni Mudra.

I will not repeat them literally, as this is a new book, not a copy of the previous one. These are all great, and you should be practicing them. We will expand a bit further on some of

---

[5] If you have health issues, or can't breathe properly for some reason, please, do not hold your breath. Just do everything but without restraining the breath. You are doing everything at your own risk. Practicing by yourself brings more freedom, but if you are a beginner, doing the techniques without someone by your side to see if you are doing them correctly, also carries a bigger responsibility.

[6] Even if you haven't yet achieved Khechari Mudra, you should still do the practices in the exact same way. The only difference is, rather than having the tongue rolled backward and upward into the nasal cavity, you will just be touching the soft palate (baby Khechari).

them though, in a more potent way, but always keeping them as efficient and straightforward as possible, and without adding unnecessary details.

The sequence you should be doing is (twice a day):

#1 **(Patanjali style)**

Mahamudra -> Kriya Pranayama -> Yoni Mudra

Or

#2 **(Classic Kriya style)**

Kriya Pranayama -> Yoni Mudra -> Mahamudra

Kriya Supreme Fire can be added either at the beginning of a routine or at the end, before the Parvastha state.

Many people have *not* been practicing Kriya Yoga long enough to safely practice the Kriya Supreme Fire technique, so I will give them here a "beginners" version of it called Kriya Bow. This technique will then evolve into the full Kriya Supreme Fire.

I will also share a slightly upgraded version of both Kriya Pranayama and Yoni Mudra, for those who are ready for an even more potent Kriya practice that will help them reach Parvastha easier. With that being said, you have the option to continue practicing the techniques your Guru or organization taught you, if you prefer. If they work for you, that is perfectly fine. Just keep in mind the goal: doing the most natural and simple yet deeply effective practice that directly leads to the effortless Parvastha state. It must also be something you love to do every day, and not a strain.

Remember that all Kriya practices *must* end with the Parvastha state of Being. That is where the most progress is made.

The most effortful, time-consuming or complex practices are the ones we should avoid. It is the mind that adores complex things. They are always a detour from the fastest path, and many times doing them feels like a chore. We are not going to make a lifetime vow of practicing Kriya Yoga. We are merely seeking to remove our false identification with what we are not, in order to recognize the Ultimate Truth that we are.

Kriya Bow

Kriya Bow is a preparatory practice for Kriya Supreme Fire. It is *always* done at the beginning of the routine, and it is *never* done together with Kriya Supreme Fire. We will start lighter and slower, and build up until we can do the full Kriya Supreme Fire.

It is pretty simple:

1- Sit comfortably cross-legged. Some people find having their hands clasped behind their back helpful;

2- Focus your attention on the Third-eye Chakra (Ajna);

3- Inhale using Ujjayi breathing (ocean breathing), moving the energy upward from the Root Chakra (Muladhara) to the Third-eye;

4- Hold the breath and bow your head to the right, nearly touching the right ear to the right knee, and mentally chant Om in the Third-eye, slowly, multiple times. Stay as long as you can in that position. Remember you will have to stay an equal amount of time on the left side and in the middle before exhaling;

5- Now come straight up and then bow your head to the left, nearly touching the left ear to the left knee, and mentally chant Om in the Third-eye, slowly, multiple times. Stay as long as you can in that position. Chant an equal number of Oms as you did in the previous bow;

6- Finally, come straight up and then bow to the middle, with your forehead nearly touching the ground (in a comfortable way), chanting Om in the Third-eye, slowly, multiple times. Stay as long as you can in that position. Chant an equal number of Oms as you did in the previous two bows;

7- Come straight up and finally exhale, moving the energy down from the Third-eye to the Root Chakra;

8- Repeat the process (2-7) with all the other Chakras:

Swadhisthana (Sacral Chakra) -> Third-eye;

Manipura (Navel Chakra) -> Third-eye;

Anahata (Heart Chakra) -> Third-eye;

Vishuddha (Throat Chakra) -> Third-eye;

And finally from the Medulla Oblongata to the Third-eye.

(Remember that except for the Third-eye [between the eyebrows] and the Root Chakra [perineum], which we use as the focal points for Ajna and Muladhara, these Chakras are located in the middle of the spinal cord, not in front of the body.)

This practice is pretty strong. Besides balancing *Ida* and *Pingala Nadis*, it is also an intense Kundalini activator. The longer you hold your breath during the bows, the stronger it will get. Beware, if you get dizzy or something similar, it is a signal that you should shorten the length of time you are holding your breath. You might feel ecstatic rushes of energy on the spine or in the head, lots of heat or even notice the body shaking. These are all just Kundalini symptoms. After finishing this practice, rest without moving for one or two minutes before proceeding.

Kriya Supreme Fire

I already shared this practice in *Kriya Yoga Exposed*, but here I will explain it a bit more in-depth.

First of all, you need to be able to hold your breath for 1 minute and 30 seconds to 2 minutes. Thankfully, by previously practicing Kriya Bow and Yoni Mudra, you've gotten better at holding it. Anyway, if you still can't achieve at least 1 minute and 30 seconds, you should do the preliminary practice throughout the day. Before doing your usual Kriya routine, try to hold the breath for as long as you can, but do not tighten up the body while doing so. Try to keep it relaxed, avoiding too much pressure. Go slowly, until you can hold your breath for 1 minute and 30 seconds to 2 minutes. Use a timer to know exactly what you can do. The preliminary practice for Kriya Supreme Fire should only be done when you are still practicing Kriya Bow, and should not be done when you start practicing Kriya Supreme Fire.

Preliminary practice for Kriya Supreme Fire

Guidelines:

#1 Don't do it with a full stomach, as this practice will actively wake up the huge fire in your belly region.

#2 Do it before practicing Kriya Yoga and whenever you can throughout the day. Do not do it while driving or in any situation that might be dangerous.

#3 Inhale only up to 80%-90% lung capacity and hold until you can do more than 1 minute and 30 seconds smoothly. Do not exceed your capacity. Go with ease.

#4 The point of attention should be in the navel zone.

#5 It might take some days or some weeks to be able to hold the breath for the stipulated time with ease, and that is fine. Be gentle and not in a hurry.

#6 You might shake and feel lots of heat, that is normal. Just don't faint and don't exceed your current ability. It will increase with practice.

#7 If the fear of death or choking comes up, and internally, you are still feeling at ease (even in the midst of such a situation) you can keep going. If not, or if you feel like you are definitely going to faint, it is better to stop.

These are the preparatory steps for Kriya Supreme Fire. My suggestion is to do them with Kriya Bow until you can hold your breath for two minutes in a comfortable manner.

Kriya Supreme Fire Details

This is a very advanced practice. Something of this magnitude would never be given in a "First Kriya" initiation.

The concentration spot should be either on the navel zone, 3 or 4 fingerbreadths below the navel, on the perineum, or on the heart space. Try each one and see which one fits you best. Always keep a straight spine and never allow your body to bend.

At the beginning of this practice, you might feel a lot of heat, then you might start shaking or having some sort of mini-convulsions, and finally, a massive empty silence will fill you up. The sheer amount of energy built up with this practice is immense.

There can be many side-effects, like rage, impatience in daily life, pain in the body, itching in the legs, headaches, insomnia, etc., but there can also be an increase in appetite, and a boost in self-confidence, willpower, and vital-energy. Above all, you might finally be able to clearly feel the Pranic/Kundalini energetic-currents. If you get too angry or overwhelmed, or if things aren't going well, go back to practicing Kriya Bow for a while and then reattempt after some days or weeks.

Doing Mahamudra and Pranayama will help you to lessen the side effects. It is the perfect combination.

Kriya Supreme Fire Instructions

1- Do Khechari Mudra, or put the tongue upward as much as you can (strive to achieve Khechari, it is important in here).

2- Inhale up to 75-90% full capacity, pulling the energy up from the Root Chakra (Muladhara) toward the Heart Chakra (Anahata).

3- Hold the breath, gently, and pull your lower abdomen in and up, and lock it firmly as in *Uddiyana Bandha* (Abdominal Lock) with *Mula Bandha* (Perineum Lock) and *Jalandhara Bandha* (Chin Lock) as well. Keep all three locks until you exhale.

4- Relax and hold the breath for about two minutes, if possible in the heart area instead of the belly area.

5- Focus on your chosen concentration spot. Choose where it feels empty and spacious (navel, 3 or 4 fingers below, perineum or the heart space).

6- You will feel a massive heat and will probably be shaking, but then... a vast silence comes. Stay with that silence as long as you can, but don't go over the prescribed two minutes.

7- Release everything and exhale. Notice how the Heart Chakra opens and joy is felt afterward. You might also feel some "ecstatic electricity" going from the Root Chakra upward through the spinal column.

8- Relax and calm down.

Do it up to three times for the first couple of weeks. Then you can increase it as much as you want, as long as you feel comfortable. Some people do it for half an hour before proceeding to the next practice.

This will burn lots of energetic blockages, and although it is a powerful practice, by having done Kriya Bow previously for some time, it will not feel too demanding for your system.

It is critical that you are proficient and already capable of correctly executing the three main Bandhas mentioned in the instructions:

Jalandhara Bandha: gently pressing the chin against the chest. Sometimes, doing Kechari Mudra along with this Lock might feel uncomfortable. Do it as smoothly as you can, and eventually it will be easy.

Mula Bandha: contracting the perineum muscles.

Uddiyana Bandha: sucking the abdominal area in and upward.

Your life-force will be building up already, and if you have not yet awakened the Kundalini, this will be the key. The Bandhas are very important, but usually take a secondary role in Kriya Yoga. Some Gurus or organizations don't even mention them.

This practice is a powerful bomb to awaken the primal energy. The intense pressure and heat waves will shake the dormant Kundalini into awakening, fiercely going up through the Sushumna Nadi. If it over-energizes you or gives you insomnia, then don't do it near bedtime. Perhaps do it only in the morning, and if you can do it twice, do the second round before dinner.

If too much energy builds up, you might need to do some "grounding work." Examples of ways to get grounded are: interacting with nature, doing physical exercise, doing asanas, eating a bit heavier, etc.

Kriya Supreme Fire is the strongest energetic practice in this book, and in most Spiritual literature. It is not a part of traditional Kriya, but it is so potent that it could not be put aside. Khechari Mudra + Bandhas + Breath-retention = sure way to awaken Kundalini if done correctly.

Supreme Kriya Pranayama

This Pranayama version is similar to the one shared in *Kriya Yoga Exposed*, except that the Oms are mentally chanted in the Crown Chakra (Sahasrara), rather than the Third-eye (Ajna), and there is the addition of a new Mudra that will make a *big* difference.

You can do as many or as few Kriyas as you want. Once you enter into a state of "Tranquility," as Lahiri Mahasaya called it (in the English translations), stop the Pranayamas and melt in that Parvastha state.

Kriya Pranayama is the most important technique in Kriya Yoga. It is also one of the most joyful and ecstatic practices to do. You will feel lots of energetic currents of ecstasy and bliss in your spine and body, especially when Sushumna Nadi opens.

I will share the practice instructions without overcomplicating them, as often happens in Kriya Yoga. They are precisely what we need for what we want to accomplish.

1- You should sit cross-legged in your normal position. No need for *Padmasana* or *Siddhasana* (unless you can do them with ease). Just a comfortable, relaxing cross-legged position. Do Khechari Mudra if you can, if not, do baby Khechari.

2- Let your attention gently go upward into the Crown Chakra, the thousand-petaled lotus. Always maintain your focus there during this practice. Don't let it go anywhere else.

3- While your attention is put in the Crown Chakra, roll your eyes upward toward it, comfortably, as if you were attempting to look at the ceiling. Do not move your head or close your eyes, let them be semi-opened. They might blink a lot at the beginning, but with practice it will become natural. Just don't strain them. This is a very potent form of *Shambhavi Mudra*, as exemplified in Lahiri Mahasaya's famous original photo. It will collect all the prana in the Crown Chakra. If done properly, your Pranayama will become an explosion of ecstasy.

4- Inhale naturally using slow Ujjayi breathing (ocean breathing), while mentally chanting Om six times in the Crown Chakra. *Your attention is supposed to be at the Crown Chakra, rather than going upward through Sushumna Nadi.*

5- Exhale naturally using slow Ujjayi breathing (ocean

breathing), while mentally chanting Om six times in the Crown Chakra. *Do not move your attention downward, keep it in the Crown Chakra.*

6- Do this for as many Kriyas as you wish, until you enter into a deep Parvastha state. It is usually done in multiples of 36 (36, 72, 108 or 144 times).

Your breathing is supposed to be very subtle and long because you will have been practicing Kriya Pranayama for quite a while before attempting this upgraded version. Sometimes your attention might go even higher above the Crown Chakra to a little known "8th Chakra." If that happens, it is okay. Let your intuition guide you.

That's it! So simple, yet very effective. It will be delightful. Joy and peace will permeate your whole body. Tears of divine ecstasy will stream down your face.

Sahasrara Yoni Mudra

This is a simple procedure, and we will enhance it from the previous version by going up to the Crown Chakra (Sahasrara) and adding the three main Bandhas.

1- Inhale deeply with Ujjayi breathing while feeling the prana going up from the Root Chakra up to the Crown Chakra through the Sushumna Nadi.

2- As soon as the energy reaches the Crown Chakra, hold the breath and close the ears with the thumbs, the eyelids with the index fingers, the nostrils with the middle fingers and the lips with the ring and little fingers. Apply the three main Bandhas, Uddiyana Bandha (Abdominal Lock), Mula Bandha (Perineum Lock) and Jalandhara Bandha[7] (Chin Lock). Keep all three locked until you exhale.

3- Mentally chant Om as many times as you possibly can in the Crown Chakra, as long as it is comfortable. Try to go above one minute, at least. You should have built breath-restraint power from the other practices.

4- Exhale and move the energy down through the middle of the spine (Sushumna Nadi) toward the Root Chakra.

Don't put pressure on your eyes, just drag the eyelids down with the index fingers by applying pressure on the upper cheekbones at the corner of the eyes.

You can repeat this up to three times, with about 30 seconds of rest in between.

---

[7] Sometimes, doing *Jalandhara Bandha* with *Yoni Mudra* can be awkward. With enough practice, everything will fit nicely into place. Be gentle and do not hurry.

Final Details

The advanced Kriya practices given here are very powerful. Kriya Supreme Fire and the upgraded versions of Kriya Pranayama and Yoni Mudra, along with the three Bandhas and Khechari Mudra, will 100% awaken your Kundalini if it is still dormant. This is an explosive cocktail, so Maha Mudra and some additional grounding work outside of your spiritual practice might prove to be an essential aid.

Sometimes, during the practice, you will naturally be drawn into a Parvastha state. So, for example, after completing Kriya Pranayama, don't be in a rush to practice Yoni Mudra. Just keep quiet and let go of everything besides your own consciousness. Simply Be. These blissful Self-attentive states, sometimes termed "intoxicating" in certain translations of older Kriya books, might indeed happen in between the techniques, and not just at the end. It is entirely okay to allow them and even recommended. Just follow your intuition in that moment.

Keep in mind that the Post-Kriya Awareness is the most important part of any Kriya routine. Even if you don't practice Kriya Yoga, you can still apply some of its principles into your spiritual practice.

What we've discussed in this chapter is the "energetic side" of the yogic path to enlightenment. We will now approach the "love side" and then the "wisdom side." All three combined together form the most powerful Yoga.

> "The most excellent part of all that is seen and heard from the continuous practice of Kriya is the Parvastha of Kriya, which is Brahman Itself. That Brahman is verily the Self Itself - Formless, Omnipresent, and Self-Experiential in Its own Nature - meaning: the 'intoxicating feeling' that automatically comes about in the Parvastha of Kriya is verily the feeling of one's Self."
>
> - LAHIRI MAHASAYA
> AVADHUTA GITA, COMMENTARY BY LAHIRI MAHASAYA

CHAPTER 8

THE ART OF NON-DUAL BHAKTI

There is a tremendous difference between practicing mechanically versus practicing with love and devotion. One will lead you nowhere, the other to enlightenment.

If you attempt to practice in a "dry" non-devotional way, it will never go as smoothly and deeply as it would if you were practicing by first feeling love and devotion toward God in your Heart. The difference will be huge! It will open the Heart and the doors of love, which will infuse the practice with much more one-pointedness, surrender, and all of the qualities necessary to go further quickly. It doesn't have to be surrender and love to God, it can be to the Self or to infinite Consciousness if you prefer, which is the same but without any apparent religious connotations. Some people prefer to surrender and be devotional toward "Mahavatar Babaji," the legendary Guru of Lahiri Mahasaya. The problem with that is that you are limiting Babaji (God) to duality and form. Unless you "see" Mahavatar Babaji as formless consciousness, it is not non-dual Bhakti, which is what we are looking for.

Now the question might arise, "How can I truly practice with love and devotion?"

By being genuine and honest, by loving your own consciousness or God as much as you can. Each day, go deeper in the love you feel for your own consciousness. It's like falling in love—the more you spend time with your consciousness, and have delightful moments with it, the more you will recognize that it is the fountain of love, peace, and joy, and you will love it and surrender to it even more. This is non-dual Bhakti, for you are surrendering and loving your true Self, instead of something external.

Try the following exercise:

Focus your attention in the space of the middle of your head for two or three minutes.

•

Now, for a couple of minutes, feel love in your heart, feel the love you have for God, for your Guru (it doesn't have to be a "living" Guru, it can be Paramahansa Yogananda or Lahiri

Mahasaya for example) or for your own consciousness. If for some reason you can't do it, then try to feel love for the person who you love the most, and then after a few moments try to redirect it toward yourself, toward your own consciousness.

•

After doing this, attempt to focus your attention back to the space in the middle of your head for two or three minutes.

•

Did you notice how much more powerful it was to focus your attention the second time around? Love seems to spread from the Heart zone toward every living cell. It gives every practice much more power. This two-minute example was just a little glimpse of the power of Bhakti and love in action. Cultivate this Love-Awareness into your practices and into your life!

Do not overthink it. It is very simple. Your sincerity will guide you. Love will guide you. It's not only spiritual practices that purify your mind, but moments of real love do it also. Having a profound insight into what is useful in your path toward enlightenment, versus what should be flushed down the toilet, for example, is also a highly purifying moment. Some actions or events purify one's system, while others damage it. Desires, intellectual arrogance, dogmatic beliefs, anger and so on will always pollute your mind.

Why do all spiritual teachings talk about the importance of love in the path toward enlightenment?

We love what makes us happy. You will never love something that does not make you happy. This means we are all a little bit selfish, because we want ourselves to be happy above anything else. Even when someone says "I love my son more than anything," it is because loving his/her son is what makes him/her happy.

Since the very nature of God is pure infinite bliss, one truly loves God above anything else. All happiness is but a glimpse of God. By understanding this teaching, we realize that love is a potent bridge *toward* God, toward our true Self. Doing spiritual practice with a powerful dedication and intention is great, but doing it with overwhelming love and surrender is what makes a massive difference.

Earnestness and sincerity are of utmost importance. When every second of your life is dedicated toward awakening, you will not waste time in useless endeavors. Being totally committed is love.

What about love toward the physical Guru or God with form?

That is perfectly fine in the beginning, but be aware that you are worshipping a form and enhancing duality and separateness. Devotion to a Deity or a Guru alone will not lead you toward Realization.

True Bhakti starts when we practice devotion to God with no motive other than our dearest love for Him. During the initial stages of such Bhakti, we still consider God to be something exterior to us, and consequently we feel that we can display our devotion only by specific actions or rituals done by our body, speech or mind. Nevertheless, no act of devotion can allow us to "achieve" the God-state or to recognize that we are already God, which makes such dualistic practices only a slow way to purify the mind and not an efficient means to "experience" God as He truly is (Self, which is pure formless Consciousness).

> "Abandoning all limited concepts, abandoning even the division between the worshipper and the worshipped, worship the Self by the Self."
>
> - Yoga Vasistha
> The Supreme Yoga

True devotion and surrender is Being. It is not uniting with God. It is being God, which is Consciousness. Again, we come to Parvastha, the "After-Effect-Poise of Kriya." Over and over again, we see that this state is the master key to Self-Realization.

All you need is already within you; you just have to recognize it. Love your consciousness, love yourself, give all your life to your true and real purpose of recognizing that you are God. Don't let your mind jump from one thing toward another, put it in one direction only: Liberation (Moksha/Salvation).

> "Settlement in the Advaita [non-duality] state removes the difference between God and the devotee."
>
> -Lahiri Mahasaya,
written in his diaries,
published by Dr. Ashoke Kumar Chatterjee

CHAPTER 9

THE MIRACLE OF JNANA YOGA

People usually think Jnana Yoga is some sort of intellectual practice that just involves reading the scriptures or continually asking "Who am I?" or "What am I?" and so on. That couldn't be further from the truth.

True Jnana Yoga is the awakening of real Discernment-Wisdom by abiding in the "I am" state, which is the same as the Parvastha state of Kriya's "After-Effect-Awareness." The only difference is the method used to reach that state. If in Kriya Yoga we use life-force restraint techniques, Mudras, Bandhas, etc., in Jnana Yoga we ask ourselves "Who Am I?" —and *feel* the answer as "I am," as that empty consciousness that underlies all experience.

We know "I exist" or "I am." We know that we exist, that we are. This sense of beingness, of existence, the sense of "I am"—

we recognize its presence in us and stay with it. This is true Jnana Yoga, or better yet, *Atma-Vichara* (Self-Inquiry).

Atma-Vichara is not about asking "From where does this world arise?", "How does suffering end?", "What is the nature of so and so?", or anything like that. That is not Self-Inquiry; that is "otherness-inquiry."

The only necessary questions are those which turn our extroverted attention back on itself, such as "Who am I?" or "To whom do these thoughts arise?" Their purpose is to revert the mind toward the background of consciousness. It is just a way to be in a Self-awareness state.

That being said, most of the time our mind is not calm enough to be able to sustain the feeling "I am." That's why we start with Kriya Yoga, rather than asking 'Who am I?' and just having the mind go crazy with thoughts and desires and so on. It is easier to quiet the mind first through Kriya Yoga, for the Kriya practices have a tremendous impact on the mind, stilling it.

Breath is related to prana (life-force) and the mind. Breath is the gross form of prana, and prana is the gross form of the mind. By controlling one, we control the other. That's why we practice Pranayama and Kriya Supreme Fire—because they allow us to control the breath, prana, and the mind.

With a stilled mind, we can proceed even further into Bhakti Yoga by adding more love and one-pointed devotion into the equation, which are both of huge importance, and then finally arrive at Jnana-Kriya Yoga's Parvastha.

> "Remaining in Kriya's transcendental state, desires are extinct."
>
> - LAHIRI MAHASAYA
> PURANA PURUSHA

Only by abiding in the Spiritual Heart as Consciousness, without any adjuncts, can we dissolve this ego-ghost that appears to be us. Although the Spiritual Heart is said to be located two digits to the right of the center of the chest, it is neither a place nor a chakra. The only way to "enter" it is by abiding and melting into the sense of Being, either by practicing Conscious-Parvastha or by staying as the empty background of Consciousness.

Many practitioners think that Self-Realization will "happen" once the Kundalini has reached Sahasrara, the Crown Chakra. After a careful self-investigation, I have found this to be false. According to my own experience and the experience of some of the undoubtedly Self-Realized Masters, such as Sri Ramana Maharshi (considered the greatest Sage of the twentieth century), the final resting place of the Kundalini is in the

Spiritual Heart. That's where we are "going." First, there will be the ascent of the Kundalini and then the subsequent descent. No true Self-Realization happens in the Crown Chakra (only temporary Samadhis), and any spiritual path that ends in the head rather than the Heart is incomplete. The feeling of "I" arises from the heart-zone and will end there.[8]

Remember that staying as empty Consciousness/Parvastha is not a thought, not an intellectual act, not a doing, but just Being. Please, pay attention to this. It's so important that the mind will overlook it as something disposable, yet it is the crux of all spirituality.

This Parvastha-Being-Presence state is the easiest of all "practices," and yet it can't even be considered a practice, as it's not a movement of the mind, but a complete halt of everything. Many people say they can easily practice Pranayamas, mantras, and so on, but they can't seem to practice Conscious-Parvastha or Atma-Vichara.

Why do they say it is hard? Is it really hard?

What is "hard" is what we cannot do, what we do not like

---

[8] This is just to give a picturesque information about the process. Not all Self-Realized beings have experienced this. It is just a perception in the subtle body, therefore still not absolutely real. Know that the real "Heart" is the Ultimate Reality, which is not located anywhere, but is all-pervasive. It is from there that everything emerges, and where everything dissolves.

and what we do not know. All spiritual practices had to be learned. We did not initially practice them, therefore we did not initially like them, for they were something unknown to us, at some point in time. Only after being told how great they were, and how we would be in eternal bliss if we became Self-Realized by practicing them, did we put in some effort to know them, practice them and love them.

On the other hand, the "Parvastha-Beingness"/"I Am-Presence" state is inherent to every human being. Everyone IS. Do you exist? Are you aware? Yes! This is natural and easy, and you didn't have to learn it because you already ARE and EXIST before attempting to learn or practice anything. This is just consciously paying attention to beingness, to being aware, to self-existence.

How do you know that you are or that you exist?

There is a sense of being, a sense of existing, an awareness of being aware. This subtle "Is-ness" is what we stay consciously aware of. This is the Conscious-Parvastha state, one that we automatically get into after correctly practicing Kriya Yoga. This is how proper Atma-Vichara must be practiced. We will use its *tricks* to help us maintain the Parvastha state when we feel like we're *losing* it (i.e., when our attention post-Kriya starts to disperse toward 2nd person objects rather than being Self-aware).

Other possible key-triggers to help us recognize this Self-Consciousness state are:

-Be aware of being present;

-Be conscious of your consciousness;

-Try to see the seer;

-Who is looking beyond your eyes?

-Who is this "I" or what does this "I" feel like?

-Feel "I exist," feel what is like to exist.

Don't just read these phrases, *feel* their true meaning. Stop with each one and feel your beingness, your empty awareness, your Self! Feeling it is being it.

We practice Kriya Yoga first because it takes us easily into a deep Parvastha state. Of course, you could attempt to go directly there without Kriya Yoga, but as we've seen, your mind will probably not let you, due to your habits of extroversion, of attention to "otherness" (i.e., lots of mind chatter where you are thinking about all kinds of stuff). This is why Kriya is such a crucial initial step. Parvastha-Self-Awareness is natural and closer than intimacy, but our minds make it seem hard and distant. That is about to change though!

CHAPTER 10

WHERE IS KARMA YOGA?

Many people think the *Bhagavad Gita* is an instruction manual for taking actions that will help our spiritual growth. The challenge is that, as body-minds under the illusion of the ego-self, when we take actions, we are responsible for the karma resulting from those actions (for better or for worse). According to the story, Arjuna refused to fight his enemies because he didn't want to incur the negative karma that might have accrued from fighting. Despite this, Krishna told him that even if he refused to take action and fight, that because he still retained the sense of doership, he would reap karma nonetheless. Krishna then told him that, until that sense of being the doer disappears, one is bound to act.

Karma Yoga usually means selfless action. My question is: can you really perform selfless action while you still have the sense of doership, the identification with your ego-self?

Karma Yoga is a consequence of Realization, not a path toward it.

> "The fruit of action passes.
>
> But action leaves behind
>
> Seed of further action
>
> Leading to an endless ocean of action;
>
> Not at all to Liberation."
>
> - RAMANA MAHARSHI
> UPADESA SARAM

Many great Sages and Yogis provided fabulous "service" toward the evolution of the world in one way or another. Look at how many great things Paramahansa Yogananda or Swami Vivekananda did. Yet they only did them after their *sadhana* period was over.

Karma Yoga can be a minor aid, but it is not really a way to eternal bliss.

For example, if we eat a peach, it no longer exists as such, but its seeds will prevail and they will eventually grow into new peach trees, which will produce more peaches and seeds. In the same way, the fruit of each of our actions will vanish once we experience it, but its seed caused by that action remains, and given favorable conditions it will germinate, prompting us to do the same kind of action again. Consequently, even after we have experienced the outcomes of any of our past actions, we will still have a tendency, a *vasana*, to repeat those actions, meaning they are self-perpetuating.

Whatever action we take will always reinforce our inclination to do the same kind of action again. Good actions produce delicious fruits (delightful experiences), while bad actions produce distasteful fruits (unpleasant experiences). It doesn't matter what kind of action it is; it will always create new karma, new seeds that will sprout and drown us in Samsara. We can never be liberated by doing actions.

You cannot do genuine Karma Yoga while you still haven't realized your true nature. If you attempt it, it will be fake, and even if you try your hardest to be sincere, the question is, are you really doing it selflessly, or with the purpose of achieving Self-Realization or of pleasing your Guru or chosen Deity?

The best Karma Yoga that you can do is to practice Kriya Yoga and be fixed in the Self. When you are empty of your fake "I," God will act through you, as you. Then, there will be no resistance to the Universe's river of life.

"The mind has merged in Brahman. Because there is no 'I,' I have no good or bad karma."

- LAHIRI MAHASAYA
AVADHUTA GITA, COMMENTARY BY LAHIRI MAHASAYA

CHAPTER 11

ALL YOGAS ARE ONE

What makes what is taught in this book the most powerful Yoga are not the Kriya techniques themselves, but the unifying of true Bhakti and Jnana Yoga into Kriya Yoga, in conjunction with the revelation of the importance of abiding in the Parvastha-Beingness state. True Self-Knowledge will not arise by practicing any techniques, but only by blissfully staying in that Self-Awareness state, which is the state we will be in as a result of correctly practicing Kriya Yoga. This is the "Final Special Kriya" as taught in the previous volume.

> "In Kriya's transcendental state, when self [ego] is non-existent, duality is non-existent. Only by constantly abiding in this state, the knowledge of Essence dawns."
>
> - LAHIRI MAHASAYA
> PURANA PURUSHA

Most Kriya Yoga, as long as it is not terribly distorted, will give similar results in the long run. I do not claim that the Kriya techniques given here are better than others taught by genuine Gurus or organizations. What I do say is that proper Kriya Yoga has the secret power to unleash the fastest path to realization, if it is merged with the other two Yogas, in their special variants as taught here. Kriya will give you the base for the other two.

If you were only to do Bhakti Yoga, especially traditional Bhakti, it would be very dualistic, which, as we've said before, would not be enough to *achieve* Self-Realization.

If you were to practice only Jnana Yoga, you might find it either too difficult, or you would probably confuse it with some sort of intellectual exercise, which seems to be a trend these days. Self-Realization is not an intellectual understanding.

If it were practiced traditionally, you would have to do the "I am Brahman" or "I am That" meditations (as per conventional Advaita Vedanta), which would be slower than Kriya Yoga in my experience. You would also spend your time reading lots of scriptures full of Sanskrit terms and outdated eastern parables. There would be a slim chance that you'd go all the way to the end with it.

The Jnana Yoga we will unite with Kriya Yoga is not the

traditional one at all, but rather as taught by the great Sage Ramana Maharshi, which is different and in harmony with the "After-Effect-Poise of Kriya." As we now know, it is called Atma-Vichara or Self-Inquiry.

By having the powerful Kriya Yoga as the basis to reach the Parvastha-Beingness state, we are assimilating the teachings of the other two Yogas (Love-Awareness and Discernment-Wisdom), making it the fastest yogic path to Enlightenment!

We are getting the best of three *worlds*. We are not attached to any tradition, set of techniques, guru or organization anymore; we take what works, and let go of what doesn't work. It doesn't matter where it originates from, for our goal is eternal bliss, God, and not anything else!

3
THE FORGOTTEN STAIRWAY TO BLISS

CHAPTER 12

SAVING THE WORLD

"Nobody is a sinner, the mind itself is the sinner when it becomes outward away from the Kutastha."

- LAHIRI MAHASAYA
YOGIRAJ SRI SRI LAHIRI MAHASAYA AND
HIS 108 PIECES OF ADVICE

The biggest "sin" you can commit is to not discover who you truly are, to not recognize your blissful nature. Constant dissatisfaction or suffering should not be accepted as part of life.

Know that the biggest gift you can offer the world is your Self-Realization. Man will always be ignorant, no matter how much he knows, if he doesn't know himself. Anything you can give the world will always be temporary, and not even all the love in the world can stop someone from suffering.

Your awakening will make you a constant fountain of true love, peace, and wisdom to all those who are open to drinking from it, leading them toward their own awakening. That is eternal. But to help others, we must first help ourselves. We must learn how to swim before trying to save anyone else in the sea of Samsara.

If there is ever to be peace in the world, Man must first find peace in himself. True permanent inner peace can only be found through spiritual awakening, which is achieved through spiritual practice.

Taking time off from who we think we are and discovering the impersonal Divine within is not an egoistic act. It is actually the road toward the end of our little self-centeredness. It is the end of egotism. Know the Unborn, and real kindness, compassion and humility will emanate from you. That is why you should practice. It is not only the end of your suffering and desire-based life, but also the opening of a door for *others* toward true happiness, toward true togetherness.

> "Change yourself and you have done your part in changing the world."
>
> - PARAMAHANSA YOGANANDA
> UNDREAMED-OF POSSIBILITIES

CHAPTER 13

THE ABYSM OF THE INTELLECT

Everything you hear or read is not ultimately true. All the greatest Sages taught the most profound teachings through their Silent Presence, which is beyond time and space. Only when the disciples failed to receive it, bath in it and dissolve in it, did the Sages teach orally or via written words.

The purpose of such words is to guide you back toward that Silence, toward the infinite Consciousness, which is Self, God. The words are just an aid, not the true substance.

> "Silence is the language of God,
> all else is poor translation."
>
> - JALALUDDIN RUMI
> TEACHERS OF WISDOM

Learning the instructions is not enough. Knowing the words and theories without the real direct experience of your true nature (the impersonal Being-Consciousness-Bliss), does not make you enlightened. We have to go beyond the words, in the direction of their true meaning.

Practice is utterly necessary. If you do not practice, you will not go further. You have to experience what this book is talking about. Just reading is not enough, only direct experience will truly satisfy your thirst.

If you lack self-confidence, don't keep paying attention to what the ego is saying. Instead, practice with full dedication, and within a few days, a glimpse of what is possible will arise and give you encouragement and hope.

Having an interminable labyrinth of either confused thoughts, or extremely subtle and clever thoughts and concepts is not Self-Realization. Knowing the *Bhagavad Gita* or the *Vedas* by memory doesn't help you in the least.

There is a time when we have to drop all acquired knowledge since it becomes an impediment. Even the most profound scriptural knowledge has to be dropped. The practice is unrelated to the concepts that people have heard, read or imagined.

Many people do not comprehend this, so I will give a simple example that will make it more understandable:

Each night, as you go to sleep, you have to let go. You have to let go of everything. Anything that you actively keep in your mind will prevent you from falling asleep. Unless you drop it, you will not fall asleep. To fall asleep, you have to surrender to sleep. If you happen to have something in your mind, it doesn't matter if it's related to something you saw on TV that you found captivating, or whether it's some profound passage from the *Upanishads*, you will have a hard time falling asleep.

In our case, we have to be empty, let go, and surrender to the Divine. Just like falling asleep, the surrender must be effortless, because if you *try* to sleep, you will only meet sleeplessness.

Reading countless books will never be enough. You must put what is written into practice, or your intellect will be polluted with multiple theories, stories, dogmas, etc., that go nowhere. Abandon all the theories and experience the truth for yourself. Drop all suppositions and assumptions and stop giving reality to concepts, which are just distortions of Reality.

The instant you begin thinking, you conceive a mental universe of intermingled words, opinions, and theories. These will, most remarkably, create, preserve and justify each other's existence, even though they are completely without basis and are nothing more than inventions of the ego-mind.

The ego is the densest form of darkness, and is the originator of all wars, murders, thefts, dramas, suffering, etc. All negative things come from this sense of separateness. When it is dispelled, the inner light of Consciousness is automatically recognized to have been there all along, ever pure and ever shining.

Just as clay can be shaped into multiple different objects, yet always remaining as clay, the same happens with Consciousness. Despite the various apparent forms it assumes, it remains ever the same: pure, indivisible and formless.

CHAPTER 14

EXPANDING PARVASTHA HOLDS THE KEYS TO INFINITY

The following quote by Paramahansa Yogananda holds a profound secret. A secret that is plainly in front of everyone's eyes, but nobody seems to see it.

> "No matter what you are doing, keep the undercurrent of happiness. Learn to be secretly happy within your heart in spite of all circumstances."

- PARAMAHANSA YOGANANDA,
HOW TO BE HAPPY ALL THE TIME

When we start having deep Parvastha states, whether these are Samadhis or deep, peaceful Self-Consciousness states where the mind is off, our ego-self will seem to cease to exist.

This is just a temporary experience, and the ego will make sure you know "he" is back. It looks like no matter how deeply we practice and go into Parvastha, the peaceful egoless state just doesn't seem to last. Sometimes it may last minutes, hours or even days, but that "pseudo-I" always comes back.

What can we do to change that?

Paramahansa Yogananda's previous quote is the answer.

As soon as we are stabilized in the Parvastha state after a Kriya practice, we have to start consciously expanding it into our daily life. You will notice that a remnant of the Post-Kriya Awareness has stayed with you, which can be recognized as deep peace, joy, love, and spaciousness. You will have to consciously be aware of it during the day, outside of your formal practices.

This is not as difficult as it seems. It is quite easy and will become effortless the more you do it. Your whole day is now a spiritual practice! All you have to do is BE.

By staying aware of that *undercurrent of happiness* that continually springs forth from your Heart, even in the midst of activities, your consciousness will start to tune into higher and higher levels of Reality, until it recognizes it is Reality itself.

Instead of living your day as "I am John, a 40-year-old

Caucasian man," "I am Kiara, a 28-year-old Indian woman," "I am Josef, a psychotherapist," etc., keeping that "I am" or "I exist" present during whatever you do will make you drop the *extra* and stay only as "I am."[9]

> "One should bathe in Kutastha [Unchanging Consciousness[10]]"
>
> - LAHIRI MAHASAYA
> THE COMMENTARIES' SERIES VOL. III: HIDDEN WISDOM WITH LAHIRI MAHASAYA'S COMMENTARIES

This quote shows the power of the Parvastha state. Everything is embodied in this little phrase. Stay over and over in the Beingness state, in the empty Consciousness, the Self-Awareness state, not just during or at the end of your spiritual practice, but also throughout the rest of the day. That will bring Freedom. That is bathing in Kutastha.

> "Perform all actions by remaining in Kriya's transcendental state or in the state beyond action [Beingness]."
>
> - LAHIRI MAHASAYA
> PURANA PURUSHA

---

[9] Do not do it if there is risk involved, like doing surgery.

[10] Refer to *Kriya Yoga Exposed* chapter "True Freedom," page 139, for a better understanding of the true meaning of Kutastha.

Kriya Yogis give a lot of importance to penetrating the star. It is a highly sought-after achievement, and many think that it will *bring* them enlightenment.

All achievements in Kriya Yoga can become big obstacles. Seek to repeat them over and over again, and you will often find yourself hitting a wall, meeting failure and frustration. "Doing" will stop you from seeing the Truth as it is. You must revert to "Being." Being is Parvastha, the state one is catapulted into after proper Kriya practice.

It is very simple. It is what is simple and natural that is certain, not what is complicated. In some ways, people do not trust what is basic and straightforward, and always go for the complex stuff. Why not give the simple an honest try?

> "God is simple. Everything else is complex."
>
> - PARAMAHANSA YOGANANDA
> AUTOBIOGRAPHY OF A YOGI

Although at first the results from consciously expanding the Parvastha state throughout the day might appear to be small and inconsequential like a tiny banyan seed, eventually, they will grow into a colossal banyan tree.

Be in the state where there are no desires, where you don't need to achieve anything.

Be in the state where there is no need for Kriya, for Guru or even for God.

Be in the state where it is ever new, ever fresh, yet immutable.

Be in the state-less state.

> "By means of an extremely courageous intellect [power of discrimination], make the mind motionless little by little; fix the mind firmly in Self and never think of any other thing."
>
> -BHAGAVAD GITA

CHAPTER 15

THE SECRET THAT NO KRIYA YOGA GURU WILL EVER TELL YOU

Some very advanced practitioners are able to reach a deep Parvastha state with one single Kriya Breath. This is a very high-level step, for all they have to do is one *Pranayama* and rest in blissful awareness, melting all vasanas/samskaras/karma, etc.

Yet there is a further step.

One day you will see through your Kriya practices. One day you will see that all of these practices are external to you, and you will ponder, "Who or what is this 'I' that is practicing all these techniques and experiencing all these phenomena?"

As you turn your gaze inward toward your own Self, you will feel a torrential flood of ecstatic bliss that will temporary engulf your "I-ness."

You will have a huge *thoughtless* realization: "Wow! It is the ego that practices Kriya Yoga! Not me! I am actually the one witnessing this illusory "I" practicing and experiencing all the phenomena!"

This recognition, which occurs after having practiced Kriya for quite a while and having awakened real Discernment-Wisdom, is of massive importance. As you will have already developed the power of concentration and one-pointedness, you can easily point your mind's attention toward the background of consciousness, going directly to the Parvastha state of Post-Kriya Awareness, *without having to practice Kriya!*

That is the moment where you *let go* of Kriya Yoga, and your "practice" is simply melting in the "After-Effect-Poise of Kriya," staying as pure Presence, as the background Witness. Object-based practices are no longer necessary, and all that is needed is being aware of your subjectivity.

> "Those who, upon having known everything via Kriya, constantly abide in the Parvastha of Kriya are the ones who are 'brahmins'."[11]
>
> - LAHIRI MAHASAYA
> AVADHUTA GITA, COMMENTARY BY LAHIRI MAHASAYA

---

[11] "Brahmin" here does not refer to the caste, but symbolically, to those who have realized Brahman.

It is a rare happening for a Kriya Yogi, and one that many will misunderstand or disagree with. Guess who will be the one who disagrees? *Someone* who has something to lose. Who has something to lose? The ego, and only the ego.

Do not underestimate this experience. It will be powerful, and it will have an immense impact, leaving a big impression on your mind. You will clearly see how limited your previous understanding was. Now, you will be seeing from the perspective of the summit, not from the valley anymore.

First of all, let's make it clear that not everyone will have this experience. It will happen only to those who have sincerely surrendered to God/Self and whose discernment has been truly awakened. If you are willing to be stripped of everything, and are ready to burn your false-self in the fire of Truth, then it will happen.

That is the end of all the movements and all the practices. It is just staying as blissful awareness, as "I am," as Beingness, as Stillness itself, throughout all waking hours. This state might even start overlapping into the dream state.

Lahiri Mahasaya said, over and over again, that the key to success in Kriya Yoga is staying in the peaceful state of the "After-Effect-Poise of Kriya." This is the turning point where we no longer need to practice Kriya Yoga to reach that state, but can instantly BE it. Why should we keep the waves of the mind undulating on and on, and continue practicing the techniques if we can directly taste the honey and dissolve ourselves in it?

"One tall rule is: In Tranquility, do not do any Kriya."

"Do not disturb Tranquility by doing lots of Kriyas [Pranayamas]."

- Lahiri Mahasaya
Garland of Letters

"When one holds onto the After-Effect-Poise of Kriya constantly, one generates Tranquility in the inner Self, and eventually he stabilizes in eternal Tranquility."

- Lahiri Mahasaya
The Commentaries' Series Vol. III: Hidden Wisdom With Lahiri Mahasaya's Commentaries

Stabilizing in eternal Tranquility happens *only* when the "I" has been dissolved.

You will never hear the words of this chapter in a Kriya Yoga initiation or book, and most probably not from a Kriya Guru either. This is especially true for those who have an organization because they need Kriya disciples to keep their organizations and followings alive. Hopefully, by hearing these words as they are laid out here, you will acknowledge what your Heart has already been silently saying for quite a while: just Being in the Heart is the key!

Very few Kriya Yoga Gurus are exceptions to what is being stated here. Lahiri Mahasaya, the father of Kriya Yoga, is certainly one of them. His words throughout these two Kriya Yoga books have unquestionably shown us so.

> "It is He [God/Self] who is beyond the beyond.
> He is beyond meditation.
> He is ever the Cause of Bliss.
> He resides as an Immaculate Crystal in the
> Sky of the Heart."

- LAHIRI MAHASAYA
GURU GITA, COMMENTARY BY LAHIRI MAHASAYA

CHAPTER 16
GIVING UP THE "I"

The mind is just a bundle of thoughts, whose primal thought is "I." "I" is the root of all thoughts. Without "I" arising first, there can be no other thoughts. "I am a man," "I am Sarah," "I am tall," "I am sick," etc., come only after "I."

This "I-thought" is the seed from where the world springs. It shoots from the Spiritual Heart up through the subtle channel called *Amrita Nadi* until it reaches the brain, and subsequently spreads throughout the whole nervous system. Then the "world" is seen. As long as one is identified with the body-mind through the attachment of this spread out I-consciousness via the life-force, one lives in duality.

This "I" is a mistaken experience of who we are, it is fake. Like in a trick of self-hypnotism, it believes itself to be an individual entity, always feeling the lack of completeness. This leads it to think it is the doer of actions, continually needing to do something or to achieve something in order to feel fulfilled, and to remove the constant dissatisfaction. But before doing, we have to be. Only by being, can doing be done, which means being is before doing. Being is impersonal while doing is personal. Whereas the first is pure, the latter is tainted by an apparent self-centeredness. Living life as Being, the world is beautiful. Living life as the doer, it is filled with joy and sorrow, love and fear, happiness and misery, etc.

Being is synonymous with Consciousness. As we've learned, the "After-Kriya" state is all about being, a Self-Consciousness state.

"I myself am only Consciousness, the Supreme Being."

- Lahiri Mahasaya
Lahiri Mahasaya's Diaries 18th August 1873

Being isn't opposed to living life. It doesn't imply that you sit and don't do anything all day long. It does mean that you simply aren't hoping for something to happen. You embrace life as it is, for life is not separated from you! Your body-mind will act and do what it has to do, but inside, you are peacefully reposing in your blissful Self-Awareness.

When we finally look at ourselves, with great love and devotion, we will smile. We will smile and laugh because we will realize how foolish we've been. We've been trying to find and experience everything besides "I"!

A lunar eclipse does not make the sun nonexistent; it simply masks it. The ego attempts to mask our divinity, our infinity, our true Self, but it is just an illusion.

If you want to remove "my pain," "my dilemmas," "my unhappiness," "my fears," "my dissatisfaction," and so on, you will never succeed. Fixing issue after issue is a never-ending job. But if you remove "I"—everything will go.

"How can one feel suffering when the mind is dissolved?"

- Lahiri Mahasaya
The Commentaries' Series Vol. III: Hidden Wisdom
With Lahiri Mahasaya's Commentaries

We have to look at what we were before we were born as this "I," before there was any "I."

What is our personality?

It is just a thought!

It is based on memories that were sculpted by our experiences and all of the "otherness"—society, friends, teachers, parents, and so on. Are you your history? Can your existence be limited to a cluster of thoughts called memory?

If we wake up with super-strong amnesia, where is our personality? It is gone, but we still exist, we still are.

For example, since you were little, every time you were shown a photograph, your parents, family, teachers, etc., pointed at your body and said "Here you are, John," transmitting the belief that you were your body and your name. Whenever someone asked you to talk about yourself, you would respond with "I am John," "I am tall," "I am dark-haired," etc.

It is this imposed identification with your body and name since childhood, which originates your personality.

Why do we still hold on to it? Why do we hold on to something as solid as a soap bubble? Is it really that valuable? Your name and story are just a big act, a concept. They are not you.

"I" is pointing at That which is conscious, That which gives life to everything, That which we really are. It is not pointing at the body or at the illusionary construct of the personality.

> "Do not think of yourself as the body, but as the joyous consciousness and immortal life behind it."
>
> - PARAMAHANSA YOGANANDA
> HOW TO ACHIEVE GLOWING HEALTH AND VITALITY

Yet we all feel that this concept we believe we are, the "I-ego," is something tangible, something real. We feel it really exists. We feel we are doers, that we actually do things. But is this true?

Do we see, or does seeing happen on its own?

Do we hear, or does hearing happen on its own?

Do we breathe, or does breathing happen on its own?

Do we live, or does life happen on its own?

Life knows how to live itself, by itself. Let's be empty of who we think we are so that Life can express itself through us, in complete harmony and symphony with the whole of creation.

When what is sentient, consciousness, connects with what is insentient, like the body, it infuses it with life, and an "I" appears between them, which is the ego-mind or ego-consciousness. It is all a hoax! We are neither this ego-mind nor the body. We are infinite Consciousness believing itself to be finite.

We can't ask the ego to give up the ego. If you try to give up the ego with your ego, it will not work.

Giving up the ego is giving up everything. That is true surrender. It might seem like the hardest thing to do, but it actually isn't because the ego doesn't exist. You don't truly exist as a separate entity. It's just a thought, an idea, based on a misapprehension of Reality.

Every night you dream of a different universe, wherein each mountain, forest, river, building, person, etc., is nothing more than your own consciousness appearing to be divided into all these phenomena. Everything there is you. In the same way, in what we usually call "real life," there is only one Consciousness dreaming this whole Universe. Each seeming individuality comes from that common source, and there is no real separation between them. Living from this belief in separation is the complete ignorance with which people live.

It is time we wake up from this mass delusion and recognize our true nature. The end of the ego is the *beginning* of us.

No matter how much practice we do, how many books we read, how many *satsangs* we attend, ultimately, when we have done all that we could and beyond, and only the last step remains, it is real love that takes hold of us and carries us through. Only with a gigantic surrender can that final step be accomplished. It is beyond all conventional or non-conventional practice. It is letting go in a way inconceivable to the mind. We are surrendering the surrender. Only that will make the Self-recognition of who we truly are possible.

CHAPTER 17

The Yogi, the Bhogi and the Sage

There were two friends. One was an assiduous practitioner of Yoga and he had a deeper yearning for the truth. Let's call him the Yogi. The other was also practicing Yoga, especially asanas, but for "fitness purposes." He had a deep attachment to his body and personality. Let's call him the Bhogi.

One day they were invited to meet an enlightened Sage to learn about Reality and the Self. They lived, learned, practiced and studied with him for two weeks.

On the final day, the Sage shared the ultimate teaching: "You are what you are looking for."

At that moment, both of them thought: "Hmm, I am what I'm looking for... What does this 'I' mean? When I say 'I,' I think of my body, so my body must be the Self!"

They both departed to their respective hometowns, and upon reaching them, they announced everyone that "Our bodies are the Self, we are the ultimate!"

The Bhogi went on enjoying his life like usual, with its ups and downs, for he had never paid too much attention when living with the Sage. Upon hearing the final teaching, he made it clear in his mind that there was nothing more than the body. Indulging in sensual pleasures was his life's mantra.

The Yogi kept practicing his Yoga, giving more emphasis to asanas, to making the body as *shining* as possible, until a few weeks later when his father died. That was a hard moment for him, and it awakened in him the feeling that something wasn't right. He decided to start inquiring deeper within.

Upon reflecting on what the Sage had taught him, he concluded that the body could not be the Self.

He saw that bodies got diseases, decayed, died, and they weren't eternal, so he came back to the Sage.

"Master, this body can't be the Self. The Self cannot die," to which the Sage answered: "Seek within. You are what you are looking for."

He thanked the Master for his teaching and blessings, and came back to his village. In the ensuing weeks, he started paying more attention to Pranayama, and to practices where the life-force plays an important role. He noticed how the life-force animates a body, and when a body dies, there is no longer life-force in it. He concluded that prana, the life-force, is the Self.

He decided to go back to the Sage, and when he met him once again, he asked: "Master, is prana the Self? Is that what you mean?"

The Sage smiled and responded: "Seek within. You are what you are looking for."

The Yogi thanked him once again and came back to his village. Upon meditating on the words of the Master, he realized that prana is the grosser form of the mind. The mind perceives prana, so it must be prior to it. He realized that the life-force wasn't the Self, but the mind was the Self!

He returned the next day to the Sage and asked: "Master, sorry for asking yet again, but is the mind the Self?"

The Sage smiled and was about to speak when the Yogi said: "No, no, it can't be Master, for the mind is in constant change, sometimes there are positive thoughts, sometimes confused thoughts, sometimes it is silent, sometimes it is restless... such a changing thing cannot be the Self."

The Sage gracefully smirked and asked: "How do you know that the mind keeps continually changing? Are you observing from a changing position as well?" These two deep questions instantly shocked the Yogi's mind into silence. Suddenly, a powerful insight surged up in his Heart.

"Master, if I were observing from a changing position, I wouldn't be able to know that the mind keeps changing because I would be changing with the mind. I must be perceiving all of this from an unchanging position!"

The Sage smiled and nodded his head.

"Well," said the Yogi, "I can witness all this from an immutable position, so the Self must be the unchanging, indivisible, beyond-the-mind, unborn and deathless Consciousness."

The Sage confirmed: "You've sought within. You are what you were looking for."

> "I myself am the Immutable Consciousness, the eternal Being."
>
> - LAHIRI MAHASAYA
> LAHIRI MAHASAYA'S DIARIES, 25TH AUGUST 1873

> "I am Great Consciousness. In the sun I saw that I myself am Brahma, the ultimate Self."
>
> - LAHIRI MAHASAYA
> LAHIRI MAHASAYA'S DIARIES, 17TH AUGUST 1873

4
TRANSCENDENCE

CHAPTER 18

THE MYSTERIES OF SAMADHI UNVEILED

According to Maharishi Patanjali in his Yoga Sutras, the purpose of Yoga is "the restraint of the *vritti* of *chitta.*" *Chitta* is the mind or the "mind-field" or "mind-pool." *Vritti* are thought ripples or "mind-modifications." *Chit*, on the other hand, means pure Consciousness—it is who or what we really are, instead of the "I-ego" we take ourselves to be, which is only the reflected light. In Yoga, we realize that our consciousness is pure, without the need for any adjunct (body, life-force, mind, or intellect).

Maharishi Patanjali basically says the complete restraint of mental activity/modifications is Yoga. The main *vritti* we have to restrain or dissolve is the *aham-vritti*, which is the thought "I." When the reflected light of consciousness ("I-ego"/thought "I") gets dissolved, either temporarily or permanently, the Infinite Consciousness will be "experienced" or self-recognized. That and only that is Samadhi, the purpose of Yoga.

There are different kinds of Samadhis, and only the ultimate Samadhi, so to speak, will lead the drop to the ocean, where it is dissolved into or united with the whole. It is called *Sahaja Nirvikalpa Samadhi.* This is the analogy normally used to describe this Samadhi, but since we know that the ocean's essence is contained within a single drop, it is better explained that the ocean-essence within the drop will recognize itself to be the whole ocean rather than an individual drop that has to be one with the whole.

Many people achieve some Samadhi and think they are Self-Realized. That is a big mistake, an ego-trap.

> "Even in deep sleep and Samadhi there is the natural gain of non-distinction (nondifferentiation/*Nirvikalpa*), however at the time of waking [from deep sleep and formless Samadhi], there is once again distinction just as before *because false knowledge has not been removed.*"
>
> - ADI SHANKARA
> BRAHMA SUTRA BHASHYA

Let us analyze all kinds of Samadhis so we can recognize their differences and determine which one is our goal.

Waking State

Mind state?

Active. Objects are perceived, there is a sense of "me" and "I."

Non-dual?

No. There is the perceiver, the act of perceiving and the perceived.

Permanent?

No. The waking state is a dualistic mind state. The mind is not permanent since it temporarily dissolves in states like deep dreamless sleep.

Dream State

Mind state?

Active. Objects are perceived, there is a sense of "me" and "I."

Non-dual?

No. There is the perceiver, the act of perceiving and the perceived.

Permanent?

No. The dream state is a dualistic mind state. The mind is not permanent since it temporarily dissolves in states like deep dreamless sleep. It is precisely the same as the waking state.

Savikalpa Samadhi (*Samprajnata Samadhi* / differentiated Samadhi / absorption with form)

Mind state?

Active. Objects are perceived, there is no sense of "I" as in a person, but there is a sense of "I" as being an experiencer. It always depends on the object of meditation.

Non-dual?

No. There is the perceiver, the act of perceiving and the perceived.

Permanent?

No. The mind experiences union with the object of meditation, but will come out of it anytime soon.

Deep Sleep / Fainted / "Unconscious States"

Mind state?

Inactive, sunk into oblivion. There is no sense of "I" or "me," there is no consciousness of being.

Non-dual?

Yes. There is no perceiver, no act of perceiving and nothing is perceived. For example, in waking up from deep sleep we say, "I was sleeping. There was nothing." But this is just said in the dual state of wakefulness, not during deep sleep. Why is it not said during deep sleep? Because there is no one there to say anything.

Permanent?
No. The mind may be temporarily submerged, but it will rise again due to tendencies and desires.

Kevala Nirvikalpa Samadhi (*Asamprajnata Samadhi / undifferentiated Samadhi / formless absorption*)

Mind state?
Inactive, sunk in the light of Consciousness. There is no sense of "I" or "me," but there is full consciousness of being.

Non-dual?
Yes. Like deep dreamless sleep, there is no perceiver, no act of perceiving and nothing is perceived. Yet there is awareness. Awareness of what? Of nothing, of just Being. It is empty awareness, for there are no objects. This is not a "dry state" though, for Awareness just being is a "state" of pure peace and bliss.

Permanent?
No. Eventually, like deep dreamless sleep, you ("I-ego") will come out of it, for your *samskaras/vasanas*, subtle tendencies and desires have yet to be erased.

Example:
Like a bucket full of water (mind) tied to a rope and left in the water (consciousness) in a well. Eventually, it will be drawn out by the other end of the rope (*samskaras*/desires/tendencies).

Sahaja Nirvikalpa Samadhi (Natural *Samadhi*, natural state, natural formless absorption, true Self-Realization "state")

Mind state?
Dissolved into infinite Consciousness, there is no "I" or "me" or anything besides pure blissful Consciousness.

Non-dual?
Yes. It is like *Kevala Nirvikalpa Samadhi*, but permanent. There is no return of the "I-ego" consciousness. This is also known as Self-Realization or God-Realization.

Permanent?
Yes. It is the only permanent "state." When the river of limited consciousness has been discharged into the ocean of Consciousness, it cannot be redirected back.

Example:
Like a river discharged into the ocean and its identity lost forever.

Now you may ask:

"How can we progress all the way from a weak initial concentration toward *Sahaja Samadhi*, our natural state?"

Unlike what many Kriya Gurus tell you, effortful concentration will not lead you all the way to the "end." The first stages of meditation, which can take any amount of time depending on the individual, will be clumsy and effortful, but eventually meditation will be recognized to be effortless. It will be a pleasure.

When the mind starts enjoying and being engrossed in what it is paying attention to, it will go from the effort-concentration phase (*Dharana*) toward effortless-meditation phase (*Dhyana*). This is just one step down from *Savikalpa Samadhi*, which is absorption with form, where the mind remains *intact*.

When there is no longer an object of meditation and a meditator, there isn't the act of meditation either, and that is union with the object of meditation. You become that object of meditation, temporarily.

By merging their consciousness with what they wanted to know, through some form of *Savikalpa Samadhi*, some ancient yogis were able to unveil every secret about creation, ranging from its grossest aspects to its most subtle elements. Some would even merge with their personal god (*Ishta*

Devata), as there are a few traditions where the final goal is union with their chosen deity. All visions, experiences, etc., belong to this type of Samadhi. Even the union with the whole Universe belongs here. But is that our goal? Will you be fulfilled with anything temporary?

No human being will ever be satisfied with anything less than the most auspicious goal. We are going a step further toward That, by which *knowing it, everything* will be known. What was written in the above paragraph is not Liberation. It is still duality. It's just a fleeting experience in the infinite space of eternity.

When we go for the eternal, we have to bypass all the distractions, all the detours and go directly toward the fundamental Reality, Consciousness itself, for nothing can exist without Consciousness, but Consciousness can exist without anything. Even God, a mere concept created by our minds, does not exist in the non-dual eternal space of Consciousness.

What we are going for is *Sahaja Samadhi*, the natural state, and nothing less. When we are "unconscious," like in deep sleep, the mind lies in the darkness of ignorance. If, on the other hand, we access deep sleep consciously (*Nirvikalpa Samadhi/Yoga Nidra*), the mind lies submerged in the light of pure Consciousness. Sometimes, this is called an "enlightenment experience."

After being in temporary formless Samadhi, there is the *knowledge* of having been in Samadhi, the coming back from it, the disruption of the body's absolute stillness and the subsequent activity, such as the observation of the mind and the life-force, and the reemerging of perception. The "I-ego" has come back.

In *Sahaja Samadhi*, there is no such distinction. The "I-ego" stays forever drowned in the bliss of *Sat-Chit-Ananda* (Being-Consciousness-Bliss). It is beyond perception, and a "state" impossible to conceive of.

Unlike the temporary Nirvikalpa Samadhi, it cannot be achieved by meditation. Throughout this book, you have come to the understanding that no amount of meditation or spiritual practice will ever "give" you the natural state. Yet we all have to start there. It is crucial.

However, mature aspirants will acknowledge that all experiences, all ecstasies, everything, no matter how deep you go, will never be enough. The persistent mind will come back. It will always come back …

… but for who?

Ponder this deeply.

You know it came back. You are aware that it came back. *You* that have this knowledge, who are *you*?

Stay as *that one*. Do not identify with the mind once again. If instead of being frustrated that the mind has come back, you disregard it and stay as *that one*, the mind will lose its power.

All the Samadhis, meditations, experiences and states have brought you here. Only "just being" remains. It is now time to awaken the ultimate Discernment, to remove the *false knowledge*, as Adi Shankara says, and unveil one of the highest mysteries you will ever find on your path to enlightenment:

It is not the mind that has to go away.

It is You that will recognize that you've never been the mind!

It was the mind that achieved all those experiences, states, etc. Whenever an "enlightenment experience" or some *transcendence* beyond the mind "happened," it was never an achievement of the mind. It was the mind that subsided and you "rested" in your pure natural Self-Awareness. Then the mind reappeared and you re-identified with it.

Now you cry that you want that "enlightenment state" back. No matter what you do, you will not have it back. It is the mind that was not present that is crying to have that no-mind stateless state back!

The mind can never have it.

Nor can it ever block it. Realize that it is here and now.

Your natural state cannot be achieved. It is ever-present. It is a Self-recognition. It is so simple, yet we seem to have to go through labyrinths of complexity and purification to reach this obvious, self-evident truth!

You are free.

You've always been free.

CHAPTER 19

THE ABSOLUTE BEYOND COMPREHENSION

The Absolute, which is usually called *Parabrahman* or *Nirguna Brahman,* is non-understandable; it is the supreme mystery beyond mysteries. What can we say about it? No words would do justice. It is beyond all concepts and definitions, beyond the mind. It is unconditioned, without attributes or identity.

Our whole apparent journey goes from the relative toward this immutable and unborn Absolute. In Kriya Yoga terms, it is a journey from Dynamic Prana (Kundalini Shakti), toward Static Prana (Consciousness Shiva).

The Ultimate Truth is that only the Absolute Consciousness, the ultimate Self, exists, and nothing else.

"The ultimate Self is Inexplicable. It is in vain to write and to say something about which is inexplicable… What else can be said?"

- Lahiri Mahasaya
The Commentaries' Series Vol. III: Hidden Wisdom, with Lahiri Mahasaya's Commentaries

True Realization does not require any confirmation, affirmation, verification or guru-given-diploma. It doesn't belong to any lineage, organization or tradition. It does not require anything from outside. True Realization includes the realization that there is no outside. There is no "other."

"When the individual self (*Jivatma*) is merged in the Supreme Self (*Paramatma*), or ultimate Self, then who will speak to whom?"

- Lahiri Mahasaya
The Commentaries' Series Vol. III: Hidden Wisdom, with Lahiri Mahasaya's Commentaries

You will discover that this Absolute Consciousness in you, is the same consciousness in me, and in everyone and everything else. What appears to be two, is *One*, even beyond the concept of Oneness. It is indivisible, immutable, not-two.

> "I myself am only Consciousness, the Self;
> there is nobody else."
>
> - LAHIRI MAHASAYA
> LAHIRI MAHASAYA'S DIARIES 18TH AUGUST 1873

> "The ultimate Self is all-pervading.
> The Self is all-pervading. Therefore, He is Truth."

> "The Lord of the universe knows Himself
> automatically."
>
> - LAHIRI MAHASAYA
> THE COMMENTARIES' SERIES VOL. III: HIDDEN WISDOM,
> WITH LAHIRI MAHASAYA'S COMMENTARIES

What does the Master Lahiri Mahasaya mean with this last quote?

There are three criteria that we use to *know* what is real. It must be self-luminous, eternal and unchanging.

Unmistakably, the Universe of names and forms (Maya) does not fulfill such requisites.

Although our mind seems to be self-conscious, it is not, since its self-consciousness is a limited reflection of our original pure Consciousness, which is limitless. The mind, whose primal thought is "I," is not present in deep dreamless sleep, nor in any so-called *unconscious* state. We do know that it is not present, for we know that we experience nothing during those states, which means we Exist, but the knower of objects, the mind, is not there.

If it is not permanent, then it is not self-luminous, eternal or immutable, for it comes (wake and dream states) and goes (deep sleep/unconsciousness states).

The mind is definitely not who we are.

What about pure Consciousness?

Pure Consciousness is the substratum where everything can appear and disappear. For anything to exist, there must be an awareness of it, because nothing is self-existing on its own, except this primal consciousness. Everything needs consciousness to be known, but consciousness doesn't need anything to exist.

This means that pure Consciousness is self-luminous, which means it knows itself, without needing any other consciousness to know it.

If there were another consciousness to know the ultimate Consciousness, then it would still be a dual state. Pure Consciousness, therefore, is self-conscious.

How can it then be known?

It can't be known. There is no knower of the ultimate Consciousness. The only way to *know* it is to BE it. The ultimate Consciousness knows itself, being.

This means that besides being self-aware, it is also uncaused, uncreated and beyond time, as we've learned throughout this book. It was never created, it ever existed, and it is eternal.

> "Where nothing whatever is born,
> that alone is the highest truth."
>
> - GAUDAPADA
> ON HIS COMMENTARY ON THE MANDUKYA UPANISHAD,
> KNOWN AS GAUDAPADA KARIKA

If pure Consciousness is self-aware, eternal and immutable, then That, and only That, is what is real.

Infinite happiness and perpetual peace can only come from That which is the absolute completeness and limitless, for no desire for anything ever surges in it, as there is nothing else.

> "Tat Tvam Asi."
> (I Am That / That thou art)
>
> - ONE OF THE GRAND PRONOUNCEMENTS IN VEDANTIC SANATANA DHARMA, IN CHANDOGYA UPANISHAD

That is "we."

That is "I."

That is "You."

That IS.

CHAPTER 20

THE LIGHTLESS LIGHT IN THE DEPTHS OF DARKNESS

I opened my eyes, and I could not see anything. It was pitch-black. There was a tremendous feeling of detachment from the rest of the world. There was not even any semblance of a world there; it was only a vague thought about to disappear.

Yet there was a light, a lightless light. It wasn't visible but I could somehow sense it, surrounded by that profound darkness.

Out of nowhere, the feeling of walking in the direction of nothingness took possession of me. I walked for what seemed to be a very long time without ever getting tired. The body-awareness feeling was dissimilar to the one I normally experience in the human form, and the only continuous similarity from the everyday world to this "void space" was the quest for the Truth that appeared to be ever-present in the innermost core of my heart.

Suddenly, two bright eyes appeared in front of me. They were dark, yet as bright as the sun in that mysterious scenario. They were looking intensely at me and I felt some energetic transmission.

Time stood still, and the eyes kept gazing in my direction. It was like a giant flaming star was glaring down on the tiny candle of my soul.

Interrupting the bubble of this seemingly eternal silence, I asked: "Who are you?"

"I am," said the soundless voice of someone or something that was so divine otherworldly, yet so intimate and friendly, like a long forgotten father. "I am ParaBrahman. I am Paramatma. I am Brahman. I am Atma. I am Shiva. I am Vishnu. I am Brahma. I am Krishna. I am Narayana. I am the Light. I am the Darkness. I am the Lightless Light. I am Shakti. I am Prana. I am the Creator. I am the Preserver. I am the Destroyer. I am the Absolute. I am God. I am the Guru. I am the devotee. I am the disciple. I am Knowledge. I am Bliss. I am Peace. I am Emptiness. I am Love. I am Happiness. I am Consciousness. I am Kutastha. I am Babaji. I am Bhagavan. I am the Vedas. I am the Upanishads. I am Silence. I am the Imperishable.

I am the Unborn. I am Deathless. I am everything. I am nothing. I am You. I am. Am."

A sudden flash of Yogiraj Sri Lahiri Mahasaya appeared before me, smiling with the most joyful yet sapient smile ever. It was from him that those sparking holy eyes came.

I started trembling and went into an immeasurable ecstasy of peace, which made a trillion years go by in the blink of an eye.

There was no darkness. There was no light. There was no Lahiri Mahasaya. There was no "I."

"I" did not go into non-dual ecstasy. It is that pure nirvanic bliss beyond "myself," beyond any concepts of "bliss," that alone IS, and I am That. It is not oblivion. It is pure Consciousness. It is *Kaivalya*. It is all there is. That is our non-dual real Existence.

Even with the apparent superimposition of the mind, there is only the permanent and effortless awareness of the Self. Shiva's motionless dance with Shakti will ever BE in the depths of the unfathomableness.

If you enjoyed this book or it helped you in some way, **please show your support by leaving a** *Review on the Amazon page.*

It will help to spread the true teachings to those who are genuinely seeking them.
Thank you.

Subscribe and receive the ebook **Uncovering the Real** plus updates and information regarding new books or articles, which will be sent about once a month.

www.RealYoga.info

If you have any doubts or questions regarding this or any of the other books, feel free to contact me at:

Santata@RealYoga.info

RESOURCES

Read also, by the same author of *The Secret Power of Kriya Yoga*:

— **KRIYA YOGA EXPOSED** [REAL YOGA BOOK #1]

The Truth About Current Kriya Yoga Gurus & Organizations. Contains the Explanation of a Special Kriya Technique Never Revealed Before.

— **KUNDALINI EXPOSED** [REAL YOGA BOOK #3]

Disclosing the Cosmic Mystery of Kundalini. The Ultimate Guide to Kundalini Yoga & Kundalini Awakening.

— **THE YOGA OF CONSCIOUSNESS** [REAL YOGA BOOK #4]

25 Direct Practices to Enlightenment. Revealing the Missing Key to Self-Realization. Beyond Spirituality into Awakening Non-Duality.

— **TURIYA: THE GOD STATE** [REAL YOGA BOOK #5]

Unravel the ancient mystery of Turiya - The God State. The book that demystifies and uncovers the true state of Enlightened beings.

— **SAMADHI: THE FORGOTTEN EDEN** [SERENADE OF BLISS BOOK #1]

Revealing the Ancient Yogic Art of Samadhi.

— **THE YOGIC DHARMA** [SERENADE OF BLISS BOOK #2]

Revealing the underlying essence of the Yamas and Niyamas. A profound and unconventional exposition on the spirit of the Yogic Dharma principles.

— LUCID DREAMING: THE PATH OF NON-DUAL DREAM YOGA
[SERENADE OF BLISS BOOK #3]

Lucid dreaming like you've never seen before. The complete alchemical elixir: Transform Lucid Dreaming into Non-dual Dream Yoga.

Available @ Amazon as Kindle & Paperback.

* * *

All the books I recommend are short, direct and to the point. They expose the truth, without fantasies. Usually, long books always have dozens or even hundreds of unnecessary pages. Here's my small list:

WHO AM I?: THE TEACHINGS OF BHAGAVAN SRI RAMANA MAHARSHI
Great short aphoristic book on Sri Ramana Maharshi's teachings.

BEYOND SHIVA: THE ABSOLUTE TRUTH
A little book expounding profound non-dual Truths in an easy to understand way.

TAO TE CHING
World known book on Taoism, full of wisdom and koans with the purpose of directing your attention toward the Eternal. I like Stephen Mitchell's version.

KRIYA YOGA - SYNTHESIS OF A PERSONAL EXPERIENCE (4 PARTS)
The story of a genuine Kriya Yogi, with many insights and detailed descriptions of several Kriya Yoga techniques.

Glossary

Advaita - Non-duality.

Amrita Nadi - Final extension of Sushumna Nadi, goes from the brain-area to 2-digits to the right of the center of one's chest.

Atma - Self. Some call it **Paramatma**, which means the Supreme Self.

Atma-Vichara - Self-Inquiry.

Bandhas - Bandhas are like valves, locks concerning the energetic system of the body.

Bhagavan - Lord or God.

Brahma - The Hindu God who is the creator of the Universe.

Brahman - The Ultimate Reality, the Absolute. Some call it **Parabrahman** or **Nirguna Brahman**, which means Highest Brahman or Brahman without form or qualities.

Chakra - Wheel/plexus, a psychic-energy center.

Ida Nadi - The left subtle channel.

Jiva /Jivatma - Individual self.

Kaivalya - Aloneness/solitude, the ultimate goal of Raja/Kriya Yoga, where non-dual Consciousness alone is.

Kundalini - Primal spiritual energy said to be located at the base of the spine.

Kutastha - "That which remains unchanged," a reference for pure Consciousness, rather than the "Kriya Star" or the Third-eye.

Mantra - Sacred syllable or word or set of words.

Mudra – "Seal." A hand or whole-body gesture performed to help the flow of subtle energies.

Narayana - Another name for Vishnu/Krishna. For some, it means the Supreme Absolute Being, synonymous with Parabrahman.

Padmasana - Lotus Pose.

Parvastha – The "After-Kriya" blissful Self-awareness state.

Pingala Nadi - The right subtle channel.

Prana - Life Force.

Pranayama - Life-force restraint/control technique.

Sadhana - Spiritual Practice.

Samadhi - Absorption, higher state of consciousness.

Satsang - Association with being, or, alternatively, being in the presence of a Self-Realized Master.

Sattvic food - Pure food.

Shakti - Personification of Kundalini, the life-force principle that gives life to the Universe.

Shiva - Personification of the Absolute Consciousness. For some, he is the Hindu God who is the destroyer of the Universe.

Siddhasana - Perfect Pose.

Siddhis - Supernatural Powers.

Sushumna Nadi - The subtle channel through which the life-force flows, located in the middle of the spine.

Turiya - The fourth state (Self-Realization state).

Upanishads - The concluding portions of the Vedas.

Vasanas / Samskaras - Latent tendencies stored in the causal body, responsible for reincarnation.

Vedas - Four collections of scriptures which are the ultimate source of authority for most Hindus.

Vishnu - The Hindu God who is the preserver of the Universe.

Yoga Nidra - Yogic sleep, retaining full consciousness while in deep sleep.

Made in the USA
Las Vegas, NV
04 April 2021